UPskill

6 Steps to Unlock Economic Opportunity for All

Authors: Laurent Probst & Christian Scharff

Editor: Lisa Francis-Jennings

First published in Luxembourg in
December 2018

ISBN paperback: 978-1-912850-66-2
ebook: 978-1-912850-67-9

The editor for this book was Lisa Francis-Jennings, the
designer was Anita Dore. Graphics designed by Sherif
Labib were also used in this book.

Although the authors have researched sources
exhaustively, we assume no responsibility for
inconsistencies, errors, inaccuracies, or omissions. Any
slight of institutions, organisations, or people are
completely unintentional.

This book was set in Luxembourg

About the Authors

Laurent Probst is a Partner at PwC Luxembourg and leads the Government Digital Transformation and Innovation activities. He is the founder and partner of PwC's Accelerator Network, building the export capacities of thousands of innovative EU companies. Laurent works with governments and international institutions, leading strategic projects focused on the adoption of digital transformation for sustained economic development. His focus is to remedy the increasing skills gap that limits economic growth potential through two major projects: EU 2030 High-tech Skills Vision and Strategy Development for the EU manufacturing industry, and the development and implementation of a national upskilling solution (www.skillsbridge.lu) for the Luxembourg government. Laurent created two coding schools to upskill and enable employment of workers in tech-related, sustainable jobs. Additionally, he was appointed as an advisor to the UNDP for the development of the Global Knowledge Index and has recently produced the Future of Knowledge Report for UNDP and MBRF (www.knowledge4all.org).

Christian Scharff is a Partner at PwC Luxembourg, leading the People & Organisation practice. He coordinates EMEA HR Technology activities and advises companies in Europe on technology and its consequence to human resource management. He is a recognised expert in the deployment of major HR ERP systems like Workday and SuccessFactors, and has worked on projects related to Rifkin's 3rd Industrial Revolution (Luxembourg government [www.tirlux.lu]), revamping university business plans (Advisory Board Member, National Research Nuclear University MEPhI [Moscow Engineering Physics Institute]), and supporting organisational CSR journeys (Inspiring More Sustainability Luxembourg [www.imslux.lu] & Luxembourg Diversity Charter [www.chartediversite.lu/en]). With his colleague Laurent, he created the Luxembourg upskilling programme and co-leads its international deployment.

Christian holds a degree in HR Management from HEC Saint Louis (Brussels) and a postgraduate degree in management from the Solvay (Brussels) Business School. He attended the Advanced Management Programme (INSEAD, Fontainebleau).

About our Editor

Lisa Francis-Jennings is an international consultant and writer. With a BA from University of Toronto (Canada), and a MSc Psychology (HEC & Oxford University) she has a strong academic background and almost 30 years' experience in business, organisational change management and communications. Her ability to explore and simplify concepts brings clients' ideas to life; creating clarity and understanding in their books and papers.

Dedication

*To our wives Christine and Laurence,
and our children
Claudia and Julia, Victoria, Margot and Arthur.
You are our inspiration today,
for a better tomorrow.*

Acknowledgement

*No concept is born in a void.
No success generated by a single person.*

*We would be remiss if we did not acknowledge those
whose ideas inspired us, provided support for our work,
and laid the foundation for this book.*

*To Leif Edvinsson and Jan Sturesson,
for their incredible energy and forward-looking
perspectives on the future of knowledge
and intellectual capital.*

*To our teams, who have worked tirelessly
to make our vision a reality.*

*To our PwC Luxembourg leadership team,
for their support with this venture.*

*To the people and government of Luxembourg,
we are grateful to have the great good fortune to live and work in
this amazingly innovative environment, where high-quality action
and ideas are prized.*

*To Lisa Francis-Jennings, who worked with us to express our
concepts clearly, so that our work is accessible to all.*

*And, last, but not least, to my daughter Margot,
who assisted with proof-reading during the finalisation of the book.*

CONTENTS

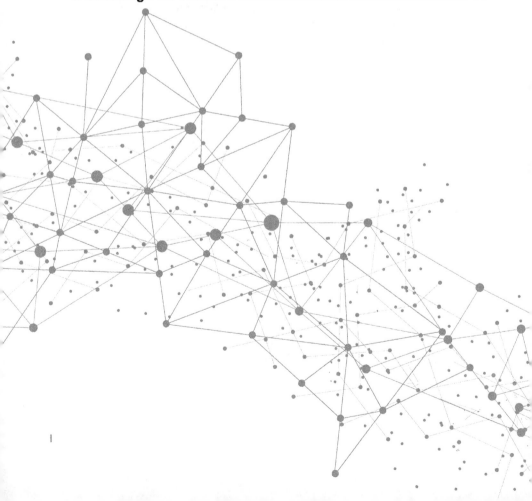

Section II
6 Steps, The Upskilling Solution

Section III
Upskilling Ecosystem Paradigm Shift

Appendix

Foreword

The Importance of Highly Pro-active Skills Policies

As an experienced member of the EU Council of Ministers of Labour, I would like to address the difficulties many governments face when trying to adapt their workforce to the challenges posed by the introduction of new technologies. New training methodologies need to be developed and the mind-sets of businesses and employees changed. While industry will have to invest in the continued acquisition of new skills by its employees, the workforce will have to embrace change and seize the opportunities posed by continuous lifelong learning. The development of new skills should be considered an investment in the future prosperity of the company/industry and not as an additional cost.

As can be observed in the case of the Luxembourg Digital Skills Bridge pilot, the aim of the government will be to provide people with a safety net while they are transitioning to a new position/job. The Ministry of Labour, Employment and the Social and Solidary Economy actively encourages businesses to define their digital strategy and to assess their skills needs. Financial support is provided to those wishing to facilitate employee mobility. First conclusions are expected to be drawn by the end of the year/beginning of next year and will be shared with other Member States. We greatly appreciate the efforts being made by the OECD to help States. Upskilling has become, more than ever, the indispensable response to the ongoing technological and economic transformation. It is an essential element of a new 'social contract' which the new technological changes require if we want them to represent an opportunity for all. Employment policies must be adapted in order to fully take into account these new developments that have a strong impact on companies as well as on society as a whole.

Luxembourg as a very open economy has made the choice of becoming an advanced digital society. This certainly means a high level of investment into digital infrastructures but above all to help citizens as well as workers and entrepreneurs to be ready for the future. To do that successfully we are convinced that confidence is key. This can only be achieved through dialogue with all stakeholders. It is the best way to make the digital society as inclusive as possible.

Nicolas Schmit

Minister of Labour, Employment and the Social and
Solidarity Economy
Luxembourg

When Your Knowledge Becomes Obsolete

As many countries anticipate stagnating growth rates in the coming years, *UPskill, 6 Steps to Unlock Economic Opportunity for All*, lays out a simple but effective strategy for human capital investment. This book offers a superb incentive for governments, industry and social society to work together to ensure not only continued economic well-being, but meaningful work for the individual.

The authors, Laurent Probst and Christian Scharff, outline key issues that influence local economies today. The straight-forward six-step summary is augmented by an assessment of innovative solutions that can be used to activate key drivers. Uncomplicated math shows the financial advantages, including the vast potential savings associated with providing a rich, rewarding technical development path for workers.

This book, describes the need to unleash upskilling potential through:

- governments fostering continuous upskilling through innova tive policies that support life-long learning

- organisations matching their digital investment with sustain able technical upskilling initiatives for their people

- markets investing in, and profiting from, funds that use sustainable approaches to optimising human capital potential

- unions, communities and individuals collaborating to form a more innovative mind-set around diversity

The benefits are clear. Progress is created or at least driven, through tipping the focus away from short-term band-aid measures. Upskilling workers in the ubiquitous technology platforms that intersect with industry today, provides a local, readily available workforce. Supporting workers to participate actively in technical upskilling delivers purpose-filled jobs that build pride. Upskilling fuels local economic growth and energises the dissemination of ideas; it is an integral component in creating a lasting foundation for global prosperity.

In an article in Scientific American Dec. 15, 2018, on the Rise of Knowledge Economics, C. Hildago asked if we are moving towards measuring Gross Domestic Knowledge as accurately as we measure GDP? This book illustrates aspects of this evolution of Knowledge Economics.

This book addresses one of the most critical but soft infrastructure issues of society today, the life cycle of practical skills and/or the sustainable span of professional knowledge. Of course, this issue is not new, but evidence is mounting that the situation is much more serious today than 25 years ago, when we started to address this at Skandia, Sweden. We are heading toward Knowledge Economics and the related challenges for all stakeholders and, most of all, for Future Generations.

With professor Paul M. Romer we addressed the power of innovation and thought leadership in Skandia. Paul M. Romer started developing his theory of endogenous growth and creation by purposeful activities in the marketplace. Romer's findings allow us to better understand which market conditions favour the creation of new ideas for profitable technologies. His work helps us design institutions and policies that can enhance human prosperity by fostering the right conditions for technological development. Romer also demonstrated how such endogenous technological change can shape growth, and that policies which are outlined in this book are necessary for this process to work well. This year (2018), he was awarded the Nobel Prize for his work on Knowledge Economics.

Society's Intellectual Capital, as well as that of organisations, is very dependent on our deeper understanding of how to effectively design and implement upskilling initiatives; 6 steps and beyond. That is what this important book is about. Intellectual Capital might also be described as the root of all fruitful endeavours. Roots are often invisible and difficult to measure. The epistemological roots of Intellectual Capital (IC) come from insights derived from the value of brain power or knowledge. The human being is surrounded by systems and technology that can be referred to as Structural Capital. Although our Human Capital is working six to ten hours per day, our Structural Capital might work around the clock; three, four or more times, in terms of productivity. The formula then becomes Human Capital is multiplied by Structural Capital (HCxSC).

But it is not only about skills, competency or the individual. It is about societal welfare. An erosion of either of these two major components will lead to an imbalance in the holistic Intellectual Capital ecosystem of an enterprise, society, region or nation. We see that this has happened throughout the centuries, mostly due to lack of understanding of strategy around human capital management and how to navigate from a longitudinal viewpoint.

On another level, it might be related to the behaviour of millennials or generation Zs, born around 1995 to 2009. They will be the leaders of our society tomorrow. With their high IT literacy causing a different attention span, learning style, and mode of interacting, we are sure to see a much more individualistic thrust to societal development and business enterprise. New models of employment, such as contracts based upon deliverables, or value creation, will emerge. Out of this, we already see the development of the GIG economy (PWC report 2018), where short-term contracts and temporary positions become the rule, not the exception.

Today, we know more. The global competition for knowledge is increasing. China is predicted to become the next scientific super power. So how do we prevent obsolescence?

We must begin to focus on continuous renewal. It is through renewing systems, both political, business, and skills that we will create the new paradigm. This is critical. We can see that our society is already far beyond Industry 4.0. We are in an era of intangibles and intellectual capital. Just look at the investment flow into fibre optics, internet, big data, coding, health, autonomous cars, intelligence defence, etc.

UNDP, UNESCO, UNEVOC, WEF, Google, Weibao and others have begun to address the need for innovative knowledge approaches. When and where will we see the Netflix of education? Already since 2016, MBRF (Mohammed Bin Rashed Al Maktoum Foundation), the Knowledge Foundation of Dubai, has collaborated with the UNDP to refine and progress the new knowledge navigation system using a GKI (Global Knowledge Index) system.

The SDG (Sustainable Development Goals) efforts will include addressing both the Human (HC) and Structural Capital (SC) within Intellectual Capital. In Skandia we started to work on these aspects in 1991 by appointing a Director of Intellectual Capital. We also started looking at the accounting and mapping systems as critical for knowledge navigation, following the development of the innovative Organisational Capital renewal tool, called Skandia Future Centre. Now these approaches have been followed globally in many nations, institutions and enterprises.

One of the cutting-edge dimensions for this pioneering societal innovation was generating Competency Insurance. This system was modelled after a pension savings plan, except using knowledge. It enabled participants to finance their knowledge renewal, when at risk of becoming obsolete. The Competency Savings System was owned jointly by the employee, employer and a third-party Savings Foundation, and supported by a governmental tax law. Up to 10% of the employee's gross salary was allowed. The savings was comprised of a contribution of up to 5% by the employee which was matched by the employer. The contribution was tax deductible for the employer, and the employee was only taxed when the amount was withdrawn for educational purposes.

The system was prototyped with Skandia staff in the late 1990´s. It attracted attention from unions, politicians and employers. Bonniers, Swedbank, City of Stockholm, and Robur were other employers that participated in the plan along with Skandia. Within a few years, the system had about 20,000 individuals participating. Unfortunately, due to political and governmental initiatives, it could not be scaled up. A clear signal that without the collaborative participation of all stakeholders (government, business, unions, associations, individuals, etc.) most efforts will be doomed.

Given the shift in the employment market, with growing self-employment in the GIG economy, it might now be a good time to launch a modernised version of this approach. It could be a societal innovation initiative (emerging out of Luxemburg)?

Leif Edvinsson, Professor Emeritus,
University of Lund, Sweden and Hong Kong Polytechnic University,
Brain of the Year Awardee, 1998, by Brain Trust , UK.

Reference: THE PRIZE IN ECONOMIC SCIENCES 2018. THE ROYAL SWEDISH ACADEMY OF SCIENCES, www.kva.se, https://6702d.https.cdn.softlayer.net/2019/10/pop_ek_en_18.pdf

GROWTH

EMPLOYABILITY   PROSPERITY

JOB

BUSINESS

GOVERNMENT

INDIVIDUAL

06

MONITOR,
EVALUATE &
IMPROVE
POLICY

Objective:
Ensure transversal
continuous improve-
ment & communicate
successes

Outcome:
Streamlined
programme administra-
tion, market alignment,
good news stories,
clear understanding of
potential jobs scenari-
os, clear return on
investment

05

SELECT
TRAINING &
PROVIDERS

Objective:
Ensure streamlined,
effective training
programme to upskill
worker

Outcome:
High level of employ-
ability & worker
motivation. Effective
collaboration between
worker, corporation,
association/unions &
government accelerat-
ed job placement

04

MATCH JOBS
& ENGAGE
WORKERS

Objective:
Match employees
(existing skills, motiva-
tion, profile alignment)
to future jobs

Outcome:
Increased employee
mobility. Upskilling
contract between
worker & organisation
with future job

03

PERFORM
INDIVIDUAL
ASSESSMENT
& ADVICE

Objective:
Assess employees,
Identify skills, achieve-
ments & motivation.

Outcome:
Cross-fertilisation.
Increased understand-
ing of employee
motivators & compa-
ny's intent

02

DESIGN
CORPORATE
WORKFORCE
SKILLS PLAN

Objective:
translate technology &
digital investment
plans into human
capital development
plans

Outcome:
forecast FTEs, future
jobs (automation), &
skills portfolio. Create
annual diversity &
workforce skills plan

01

ANALYSE &
DEFINE
UPSKILLING
INITIATIVE

Objective:
Define the upskilling strategy
of a territory, industry or a
corporation. Preparatory steps
are an essential element in the
success of any upskilling
initiative.

Outcome:
Precise scope, budget,
implementation and
stakeholder engagement plan

Figure 01: Upskill! A 6 Step Solution

Introduction: Time for Action

If ever there was a time for government, business and social society to work together, it is now. This book looks at the alarming skills shortage, the increasing demand for talent and the high vacancy rate in technical jobs throughout the Western world. The frightening implications of this continuing trend coupled with unemployment – especially in youths and older workers – is not to be dismissed. This book affords the reader a view of the 'organisational pain' being produced by massive layoffs triggered by skill obsolescence in industries that are falling short in recruiting resources for key and critical jobs.

These trending factors are causing governments to reconsider their structures, policies and systems. The elements that comprise this unprecedented challenge include:

1. high percentages in NEET (Not in Employment, Education or Training) – leading to a disenfranchised and demotivated youth

2. vocational training inefficiencies and wasted training funds – caused by participation in knowledge or skills acquisition in the wrong domains

3. higher unemployment insurance – increasing subsidy and support costs, and impacting mental health and well-being in a large segment of the population

4. losses in the tax base and revenue – impacting regional economic well-being (personal and corporate tax loss) caused by vacant positions, and migration of jobs and industries to regions or countries where skilled workers are more available.

About this Book

Our hope is that this book hastens the adoption of our radical vision of government, business and society working together, in lock-step, to ensure a brighter future for all. We also hope that you enjoy reading the concepts and examples we have compiled here. To that end, we have moved all references to the Appendix in the hope that you will have a stress-free, uninterrupted and enjoyable read.

Gravest of Situations (Section I)

In Section I, we look at the early warning signs presenting themselves in most developed countries. <u>Overqualified</u> workers are jobless; their skill-set or experience not suited to the jobs available[1]. Large numbers of youth, emerging from years of unfocused education (not tied to market projections or needs), are finding themselves unemployed and unemployable. The Middle East, where 60% of the population is under 25, sees a growing educational gap in soft skills and STEM (Science, Technology, Engineering & Mathematics) subjects. The impact on business revenue and GDP, as populations migrate and businesses move, is undeniable. Faced with a new marketplace reality, Ministries of Labour, Economy and Education are finding that what worked in the past is beyond inadequate; that curative solutions for unemployment are ineffective. They must now find a balance between offering 'the expected' support to unemployed workers, while providing visionary leadership for upskilling toward the ephemeral 'future jobs' perspectives.

Finally, we look at HR as it becomes integral to strategy setting and implementation. Management is realising that HR is one of the most strategic departments in the company. The cost of not upskilling the employee population is massive. A recruitment manager in a large French utility company, sums it up effectively,

"I now understand that we must change our recruitment criteria. We have spent much time investigating hard skills (eg accountancy), but we must now look at soft skills and the ability to learn and grasp new knowledge, so that we build a workforce that can evolve into the new jobs we cannot even forecast today."

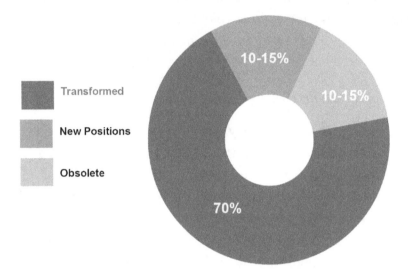

Figure #02: Automation of Jobs

The message in the first section of this book is clear: **Change now ... or become obsolete.** Government, business and individuals must work together to implement a holistic and sustainable solution. Distributing power and accountability between these groups will combat the widening gap between obsolete workers and the market's demand for workers who can fill new jobs.

6 Steps, The Upskilling Solution (Section II)

Fundamental to every journey is a map that points the way. Section II explains a solution that is already being used by a few visionary governments and businesses to: 1) alleviate economic stress, 2) address current challenges, and 3) rewrite the predicted pessimistic future. Communication is integral to the successful implementation of upskilling initiatives, and the heart of this model. Like most organisational change initiatives, engagement and accountability are central to success. This type of initiative requires government, business and individual workers to question their habits. Working together to create sustainable economic opportunities and jobs, demands that leaders and sponsors act as role models. Everyone has a part to play. Each group must take steps to align strategically to ensure full and meaningful use of resources. In the Return on Investment chapter, we provide details regarding the savings garnered by strategic investment in upskilling – for the company and government. The savings are not insubstantial; every €1 spent to upskill an at-risk worker nets out €2 in savings and revenue generation.

Our roadmap is built on simple principles. Anyone who has organisational development or change management exposure will recognise and embrace the familiar operational elements. This approach obliges key stakeholder groups to put away ineffective agendas and antagonistic strategies. It compels everyone to have conversations that create understanding and buy-in for the new paradigm.

Section II provides enough detail and examples for any group to establish an upskilling initiative in their region. For the visionary few who understand that a sustainable and continuous upskilling model is our only recourse, this section outlines key activities, milestones and also provides notes on rationale for each step. This roadmap aligns and shifts the goal posts to ensure easier and quicker implementation.

Upskilling Ecosystem Paradigm Shift (Section III)

Throughout history, we have dismissed thousands of inventions and new systems as not feasible or even impossible. Yet no matter how phobic we are, or the breadth of change we must undertake, eventually we realise the value of taking a different, more effective approach. Some readers may not believe that people can come together to work for their own greater good. Section III is all about dispelling that belief. It delivers the good news of upskilling. It furnishes details regarding some of the most important elements associated with upskilling and ample examples of how upskilling is working around the world.

Stakeholder Actions			
	Strategic Action	**Tactical Action**	**Alignment Actions**
Government	Stop short-term fixes for unemployment. Create, publish & continue to update a national skills strategy.	Put in place supporting tools (skills banks), structures (pre-financing options), policies & systems (posting national high-need job categories internationally to attract migrants).	Align all government bodies (education, labour, economy) to predict & support future jobs fulfilment.
Companies	Stop 'shotgun' or 'one-size-fits-all' approaches to training. Focus on long-term employability & meaningful work.	Identify at-risk employee populations & provide intense upskilling (increased internal & external mobility).	Commit to agile upskilling practices. Continuously communicate regarding the importance of learning & upskilling to encourage stakeholders. Urge employees to take responsibility for their career.
Workers	Create an upskilling framework for the company. Consider at-risk populations & link them to short- & mid-term projections & goals.	Describe job openings in terms of skills required. Develop/ use tools that project job vacancies & future skills gaps.	Connect to & use the government's skills strategy & skills bank frequently.

Table #01: Stakeholder Actions

The numbers are clear. This model, correctly implemented, allows companies and countries to be more competitive, as well as save corporate and tax-payer funds. It improves GDP, empowers the underrepresented, and attracts commerce and industry to job centres of excellence. It even, in an indirect manner, strengthens democracy.

Upskilling Defined

The origins of the word 'skill' can be found in Old Norse (skil), Icelandic and Faroese (skilja), and Swedish (skäl), from as early as the 12th century. The root meaning implies an ability to assess something critically; 'power of discernment', 'ability to make out, adjustment', 'to separate; understand'. Most dictionaries define 'skill' as the knowledge and ability that enables one to do something well; expertise, or type of work or activity which requires special training and knowledge. In America, it is even more focused on outcomes: 'great ability or proficiency; expertness that comes from training, practice, etc'. As a verb, *skill* implies training a worker to do a particular task.

Interestingly we see in these definitions, three thought-provoking notions: knowledge, ability, and quality of outcome. In the past, the word skill related specifically to the acquisition of applicable knowledge and a person's ability to transform it into real know-how. Craftsmanship was synonymous with this concept of superior work. For example, the quality of the cut of a diamond is linked to the skill of the craftsman.

Although skill continues to be associated with craftsmanship and manual work, today it is used to describe a high level of excellence, distinct from knowledge, in a variety of professions (both for blue- and white-collar workers) and is recognised by a diploma or professional certification. It adds the layer of 'ability to perform an activity or task effectively' that goes above and beyond knowledge.

Upskilling or Reskilling?

For most people, 'reskilling' is associated with difficult situations in which people lose their jobs during specific crises or unfortunate business catastrophes and require retraining to find a new one. Its negative connotation is associated with a small, unemployable group of under-qualified workers who lacked abilities. For example, during World War II, millions of American workers were reskilled to fill vacancies in military manufacturing. In the 70s, the iron and steel industry crisis led to imagining different solutions for people; one solution was reskilling.

Using the word 'upskilling' allows us to clearly delineate from reskilling and its negative implication. Upskilling suggests a worker's clear intent to expand capacity and therefore, employability; to advance and progress their competency portfolio, including technical, soft and digital skills. By upskilling, an employee can offer more to a company and their employment would generally be more interesting and sustainable. In the OECD Report on Automation, close to 40% of all employees in Germany have undergone at least one occupational re-qualification for professions with systematically lower risk of automation[2].

Upskilling implies re-qualification, which is an important tool in the transition to jobs that are less likely to be automated. Upskilling, as well as indicating progression, also suggests a more positive dimension and better situation for the future. This is very important in terms of employee buy-in. When tested with corporate HR directors *and* employee groups, there was a clear preference and positive reaction to 'upskilling' rather than 'reskilling'.

Finally, our underlying premise is that today realistically, the entire workforce will be required to expand or augment their skills regularly. Upskilling means a lower dependence on market conditions and increased added-value for the individual. It indicates a more positive future situation and therefore is more appropriate in this context. 80% of CEOs in the last PwC survey, clearly indicated a concern with talent availability and their feeling of accountability for ensuring that current workers are requalified regularly[3]. Thus, upskilling is more appropriate to use in this context than a word originally associated with just a small group who have lost their jobs.

Section I:
Upskilling Rationale

KEY CONCEPTS

Individuals
- Labour market shift to freelancer
- Jobs & organisations are becoming obsolete
- NEET: the lost generation

Government
- Upskilling challenge to government: a perfect storm of unskilled workers and unfillable jobs
- Government & corporations do not have robust skills strategies
- Increasing skills gap causes high structural unemployment level and vacant jobs

Organisations
- International talent war – a seller's market
- There is a better solution than lay-offs
- Technology investment must include workforce planning
- Creates high ROI for the company

Chapter 1: Realities of The Digital Age

Today technology is invading both our private and professional lives. The ongoing acceleration of new technology enables drastic productivity improvements but is challenging both individuals and corporations. We are being forced to learn an ever-growing number of applications. We must adapt to new, and increasingly frequent, technology and system updates as the digital revolution becomes a fixture in our daily lives. At the same time, some elements of almost every job in the marketplace are being transformed or usurped by innovative hardware and/or software solutions. This acceleration of the 'technologically unfamiliar' is intensifying the challenge of finding people who are qualified to fill openings, and capable of working in the shifting digital landscape. It is transforming not merely the workers' profiles but the organisation itself.

Velocity of Technology Development

In the last century, the development and introduction of technology was rather slow. It took over 150 years to go from the invention of the first commercially viable steam engine (Thomas Newcomen, 1712), to the first successful internal combustion engine (Etienne Lenoir, 1859), and finally to a more modern version (Nicolas Otto, 1876). Progressing from celluloid (Parkesine,1856) to the first digital camera (Steven Sasson, 1975) also took over 100 years. Lately, we have seen some impressive progress, with the evolution of many technologies in a single work generation. Possibly one of the most striking, certainly the most recognisable technology advance was the move from being earth-bound to manned space-flights. In under 60 years, we went from the first manned flights (Wright Bros, 1903), to the invention of the jet engine (patented by Hans von Ohain in 1930, it did not fly until 1941), to a manned spaceflight in 1961 by Russian cosmonauts.

In 1965, Gordon E. Moore, in his eponymous law, observed that the number of transistors on integrated circuits double every two years. This indicates the pace of growth in the quality computing power, storage capacity and efficiency. 40 years ago, in the 1980s, we saw the advent of the personal computer. In the last two decades we have gone from the invention of the 'mobile phone' to the ubiquitous smartphone (hand-held computer). Although it didn't exist ten years ago, it is now owned by over 2.5 billion people world-wide.

While developments of this magnitude would normally occur every 10 to 15 years, in the last decade the pace of change has accelerated to a two- to four-year cycle. This acceleration is not just challenging workers to adapt at an always faster pace, it is also threatening organisational direction, mission, and job stability. Unlike past decades, where only individual elements of the organisation were impacted by changing technology, today, this evolution impacts everything about the organisation, everyone in it, and the associated value chain.

According to the OECD (Organisation for Economic Co-operation and Development), 30% of current jobs in member states are at stake due to automation[4]. On the other side of the coin, the Belgian Prime Minister was asked why their 2018 GDP growth rate was suffering at only half that of other OECD countries and far below some other EU economies. His response was that over 130,000 jobs remained vacant in Belgium[5]. What percentage of this is caused by lack of technical skills or required competencies that do not exist in the workforce?

The EU white paper on the Growth of Europe (2017), estimates a potential gap of 700,000 IT workers in the EU by 2025-30[6]. If countries and companies are not able to source talent capable of running their factories, processes and sales, competitors elsewhere in the world will. Our new market is driven by competencies and the ability to quickly acquire technical skills.

The <u>Transformative Technologies and Jobs Of The Future</u> report, published for the G7 Innovation Ministers' meeting in Montreal, Canada (2018) shows predictions, derived from a Frey and Osborne <u>paper</u>, regarding the average risk of automation by industry[7]. It indicated that about 47% of jobs, especially those in service-provision, transportation, logistics, administrative support and production, are at risk[8].

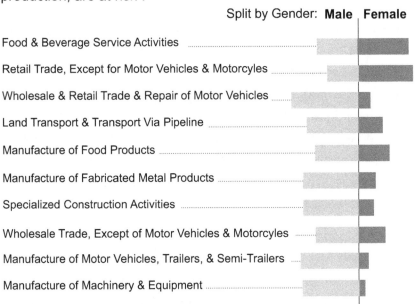

Split by Gender: **Male** **Female**

Food & Beverage Service Activities

Retail Trade, Except for Motor Vehicles & Motorcycles

Wholesale & Retail Trade & Repair of Motor Vehicles

Land Transport & Transport Via Pipeline

Manufacture of Food Products

Manufacture of Fabricated Metal Products

Specialized Construction Activities

Wholesale Trade, Except of Motor Vehicles & Motorcycles

Manufacture of Motor Vehicles, Trailers, & Semi-Trailers

Manufacture of Machinery & Equipment

Figure #03: Average Risk of Automation/Industry

Source: OECD (2017e), "Going Digital: The future of work for women",
https://www.oecd.org/going-digital/Going-Digital-the-Future-ofWork-for-Women.pdf.

We are in a time of high variability, high disruption and high volatility. 'Protected' playgrounds are not only being attacked by direct competition, but also by new entrants leveraging their technological advantages. Business models are blurring between sectors, as new entrants like Apple Pay or WeChat in China upset the existing payments service industry. Other enabling technology is causing (or in some cases, forcing) businesses to evolve. Telco's are performing distance-medical intervenes in Africa and South America. Tech companies, like Cisco, are developing and offering huge educational curricula, and Alibaba is becoming the top money market fund in China. Even hair dressers, in a traditionally low-tech industry, are beginning to use smart mirror technology to perform hair style diagnostics, easily showing a specific hair style or colour on their client.

This increased focus on technology systems, is sparking another trend. Organisations are incorporating digital into their strategic plans. The number of Chief Digital Officers (CDOs) is growing as companies realise the importance of this role. CDOs and their teams develop and introduce new technology to improve productivity through automating jobs. They insert technology that increases client satisfaction through faster reaction time and better response time to requests. ICT and the CDO use digital avenues to launch new products. This is all ground-shaking.

The list continues in the office; automated client interfaces classify client requests, offer automated answers via chatbots, determine the potential availability of sales-people for calls and establish client profiles. Sales representatives take orders on tablets, where client information such as last quarter's purchases and consumption trends are available at their finger-tips. Real-time figures allow them to know the exact moment to adjust pricing and to create tailored promotions for merchandise. Tomorrow, sales people will even become more productive and travel more safely thanks to autonomous cars and trucks.

Robotic Process Automation (RPA) is being used for many repetitive tasks associated with accounting, blockchain, and to secure data for sensitive topics like parts in the health industry or product origins for prepared foods. In the field, technicians wearing augmented reality (AR) 3D goggles, share what they see with specialist working remotely, and perform repairs based on advanced diagnostics only possible with the advent of recent tech evolutions. On the shop floor, smart factories are making extensive use of Industry 4.0 concepts like data monitoring, analysis of robot speed, raw material consumption, labour costs, and quality. Temperature is managed via Internet of Things (IoT) wired devices. IoT has also allowed the advent of 3D printing, predictive maintenance, automated conveyers and warehouses with automatic guided vehicles (AGV) … to mention just a few time-saving advances.

A clear sign that the current trend will continue is the relentless testing and adoption of new tools. Interfacing new tech with company ERP systems is becoming the norm. Organisations are investing large amounts of funds in technology because it's strategic. Yet they have hit a wall. Lower and lower numbers of qualified workers delay production and product development. This shortage causes sales to decrease, impacting the bottom-line. To address their shortfalls in the talent market, companies use wage augmentation and other strategies to steal each other's staff, which fuels even more personnel 'volatility'.

Studies across Europe reveal a shocking picture of the current technological landscape. 14% of jobs suffer from a very high risk (70%+) of being automated. An additional 32% of the remaining jobs have a high probability (50% to 70%) of being partly automated or face significant changes to their content[9]. According to the 2017 Report on Employment Orientation, 35% of the working population in France has no, or very limited, digital skills, and a full 40% of French workers who have not completed their BAC, are at high risk of losing their jobs due to automation[9].

Technical competencies, creative problem-solving and collaborative skills are becoming the most important success factors in the workplace. They are an integral component in the strategic agenda of most companies, but the OECD Report on Automation (March 2018), indicates that a mere 31% of at-risk employees (job loss through automation) had received professional training in the past 12 months[2]. On average, these employees only received 25 hours of training per year as compared with the 59 hours enjoyed by the least exposed employees. This is a clear indication that training is focused on those who need it least. Exposing populations that have a higher than average chance of unemployability, are receiving less or, in some cases, going without. All the while, there is an ever-expanding gap between competencies that are available on the market and those which are needed.

Shrinking Talent Pool

The problem of not being able to find the right talent is reaching critical proportion. But why is this happening? While demand is reaching peak levels in most economies; many countries such as Japan and most of Europe have had low birth rates for decades. The declining percentage of 'young' (children aged 0 to 15 years) is occurring in tandem with a growing 'elderly' population (population over 65). There is great doubt whether younger generations will have the time, training, or the motivation to take over the millions of high-skilled jobs left behind. Indicators include:

1. **OECD countries**: the young population decreased from a low of 29% (1970), even farther to 18.4% (2014)

2. **France**: the elderly population has moved from 13% to almost 18%

3. **USA**: the majority of baby boomers will be retired by 2030, moving the elderly from 9.8% to 14.5% of the population. The birth-rate is tumbling. This category (0 to 15 years) has moved

from 27.8% (1970) to 19% (2014) of the population

4. **Japan**: the percentage of young people stood at a low of 12.9% (2014). Conversely, the elderly population increased from 7% to 25%

5. **Globally**, the 2017 UNFPA statistics for people aged 60 or older paints a clear picture[10]

   - In 1990, there were 500 million people who were 60 or older. In 2017, there were 1 billion in that category. This figure is forecast to reach 2.1 billion by 2050

   - 5.4% of the population falling within the 70+ age category in 2018, will grow to represented 11.2% of world's population by 2050

   - At the same time, the percentage of active population (people between 20 and 69 years) will drop sharply in most production and research countries

In a booming job market, these figures are cause for alarm. Demographic shifts are clearly a growing issue in most OECD countries. For most companies, talent pools will shrink in proportion to the ageing population. In some countries like Japan, Singapore, Korea or Southern Europe, there will be more than a 10% drop in the active population. Only two countries on this list have stable or increasing active populations right now; India and Israel. The rest of the world will see a decrease in available talent and will face the challenges associated with an ageing workforce.

It wasn't very long ago that workers anticipating retirement, would slow down as they approached 50 or 55. For many today, this way of working will shortly be, or is already, history. In 2016, the effective average retirement age, with very few exceptions, was over 60 in OECD countries (OECD Pensions at a Glance). There are even more changes to come on this front. Countries like Japan are moving the retirement age at 70. The Netherlands will link retirement to life expectancy after 2022[13]. This means that those who entered the workforce at age 20 in 2016, are unlikely to retire before 71… and life expectancy is on the rise. The 25 years between 1983 and 2008 saw an increase of six years in average life expectancy (OECD Health stat). Companies will be forced to invest sizeable amounts of time and money to ensure that workers are able to adapt to new ways of working and new technologies throughout their longer careers. Recruiting will become more and more challenging.

	Percentage of Active Population					
	Ages 20-69			Ages 70+		
	2015	2050	Delta	2015	2050	Delta
World	60.5	60.6	0.1	5.4	11.2	5.8
Europe	66.8	58.6	-8.2	12.4	21.4	9
Russia	69.4	62.0	-7.4	9.4	15.3	5.9
Sweden	64.1	58.8	-5.3	13.4	19.1	5.7
Spain	66.8	53.5	-13.3	13.8	29.7	15.9
Italy	65.3	53.7	-11.6	16.2	28.7	12.5
UK	64.1	58.7	-5.4	12.5	19.8	7.3
France	62.8	56.5	-6.3	15	21.4	6.4
Germany	65.9	58.2	-7.7	16	24.4	8.4
North Amer.	64.7	59.9	-4.8	9.8	17.3	7.5
China	70.6	61.6	-9	5.9	19.7	13.8
Japan	63.8	53.3	-10.5	18.5	29.8	11.3
Korea	71.2	55.8	-15.4	8.6	28.2	19.6
India	58.5	65.7	7.2	3.4	8.7	5.3
Singapore	71.1	58	-13.1	7	26.8	19.8
Israel	57.0	57.5	0.5	7.4	12.8	5.4

Table #02: Percentage of Active Population
Source: OECD data

Constricting Immigration

There has never been a more challenging time for HR professionals. The last PwC CEO Survey showed that already today, over 45% of CEOs are concerned that there is great potential that digital skills may be unavailable in their workforce. Turnover is also a worry, with 50% of CEOs struggling to find digital talent. Finally, a full 80% are concerned with the availability of key skills for their company[3]. This is a shocking comparison to the figure of 51% in 2011, but quite understandable when we take into consideration all the data at our disposal.

Another aspect of the new reality is the wave of strong protectionist border policies. The Winter 2017 cover story _Will Stronger Borders Weaken Innovation_ for Strategy+Business, uncovered some interesting statistics on immigration, restrictive policies and creativity[12].

> _"The UK Brexit decision in June 2016, followed by the election of President Donald Trump, on his 'America First' platform, and the high proportion of multilateral agreements rejected in the last 2 years (eg Iran, EU-US, China-US) also have immediate consequences on talent migration. Our current innovation models are based upon an almost free flow of money, information and talent. This model is clearly at risk today._
>
> _Immigrants in the USA only make up 16.9% of the overall workforce, but they hold an outsized share of jobs in the high-tech, science and engineering sectors. They account for 32% of workers in computer- and mathematical-related positions according to the Migration Policy Institute.[12]"_

While we might be able to turn a blind-eye to a single source, multiple references and research corroborate that the decrease in immigration may indeed adversely impact economies. Results from a survey conducted in March 2017 by the American Association of Collegiate Registrars and Admissions Officers, indicate that 39% of institutions have seen a significant decline of between 10% and 30% in international applications over the previous year. In the UK, Cambridge reported a drop of 17% in EU undergraduate applications between 2017 and 2016.

Clearly, some understand the danger. In 2016, Scotland announced that students from EU countries who start their course during the 2017-2018 academic year would not be charged tuition fees. This measure was prolonged post-Brexit, to ensure EU students still come to study in Scotland[13]. Australia recently announced that it will allow a three-year extension to tourist visas, contingent on the visa-holder working at least six months in a rural area. This policy is specifically aimed at resolving the endemic worker shortage there. Japan, too, is signalling that it will soon soften its immigration policy as it struggles to resolve its tight labour market. In a highly competitive employment market, less talent migration is not good news for most companies.

So being a worker today is not that easy. Technology, digitalisation, and new ways of working are all impacting general competencies at an unheard-of pace. Companies are investing in training for the workers who already have the skills to 'survive' rather than high-risk employee groups who are likely to be left behind. This scissor effect is impacting our capacity to recruit new talent at a time when business is desperate for workers who can keep up with the rapid introduction of new technology. And it's happening everywhere. We observe the exact same cycle in countries around the world. The new paradox is that countries or regions suffer with unemployment, while business struggles to find suitable workers to fill vacancies. Add to this, the growing preference for freelance work and we see shrinking talent pools where employers have traditionally expected to find most of their full-time talent.

The Domino Effect of Unemployment

The political community recognises that upskilling is a critical global topic. An abundance of recent research provides evidence of a skills shortage in the jobless population, while organisations struggle to fill high-demand jobs. In the USA there were more jobs than workers available (April 2018):

1. vacant jobs reached an all-time high of **7.195** million

2. unemployment stood at 4% (**6.56** million workers)

3. wages hit an all-time high in all categories – from low- to high-skilled workers

In Japan (August 2018), unemployment reached a level not seen since 1974. A low of 2.4% meant that there were 164 jobs on offer for every 100 workers[14]. In the EU28, the job vacancy rate in Q1 2018 reached an average of 2.2% (Eurostat). It was 3.5% for Belgium and 2.9% in Germany; quite a high percentage for these countries.

Two in-depth white papers were presented at the 2018 World Economic Forum: *Towards a Reskilling Revolution*[15], and *Eight Futures of Work*[20]. These papers examined the broad implications of Artificial Intelligence (AI) and automation technologies on the global economy. The goal was to provide individual workers, companies, and governments with the tools necessary to begin thinking about reskilling pathways and job transition opportunities. The OECD has shifted a major part of its staff to work on this topic. It has opened several fellowships on the future of work. The European Commission has also been looking at this topic for years, producing several white papers and books.

Finally, most research and strategy firms are weighing in with surveys and studies on this topic. PwC's *Future of Work, A Journey to 2022*[17], Mc Kinsey's *Future of Organisations series*[18], and Bain's *Workforce of the Future*[23], are just a few that link adaptable, technology-based capability, soft skills development (such as innovation and creativity) and complex problem-solving, with employability. We see many who expect this new tech wave to consistently include massive layoffs. From the attention it garners, it is certainly a critical problem for the State, especially since forecasts indicate that the middle class will be most impacted. This wide-spread job loss will not only cause issues for individuals and families but could potentially change the social balance – which is the foundation of democracy. Many countries have spotted its importance. It has led to the:

- development and publication of the Norwegian Strategy for Skills Policy 2017-2021[20-]

- launch of a Canadian Skills Strategy that provides, among other incentives, a 2-week work permit process for highly skilled workers and a dedicated service channel for organisation intent on bring large investments to Canada[21]

- appointment of a High Commissioner for Competencies and Inclusion in France[22]

- creation of special taskforces in the USA; 'Reskill the US Worker'[23] and apprenticeship expansion to promote apprenticeships in sectors that are at risk due to insufficient workers[24]

- allocation of a personal training budget for each worker in Singapore[25]

- design of a competency plan for Bade Wurttemberg Land, followed by the set-up of training factories[26]

- increase in unemployment benefits and personal or group career guidance via specialised agencies and outplacement plans in many countries

In fact, in the last decade, most countries have developed variety of incentives to encourage people to get back to work, and for employers to hire, train, and help employees manage their careers. States and communities have been quite active but are experiencing different levels of success with approaches aimed at addressing these widespread issues. Practically everyone, both in business and public spheres, acknowledges that this topic is key for our future.

Main Messages

Knowledge obsolescence is now a tangible issue for economies and companies. It carries the risk of massive layoffs while at the same time, difficulty in finding qualified people for specific areas can mean that many jobs remain vacant indefinitely. The impact on business and national economies cannot be underestimated. The convergence of these factors could generate disastrous social and economic effects if not addressed properly. If organisations are to confront these challenges effectively, management, the CEO and the whole C-Suite, must be conversant in every aspect of their business and market variabilities in their sector. They must understand, in detail, how their organisation and the market, are being influenced by technology and by changing market needs. We have a somewhat unique convergence of economic, technological and workplace factors today.

- New technology introduction is accelerating in both business and social settings

- Most economies around the world are performing better, yet the massive migration of workers has diminished

- Populations are plummeting in developed countries, but increasing in emerging markets

- Low-level, repetitive jobs are at high risk of becoming obsolete. Some are already being replaced by automation, pushing thousands of workers towards the unemployment line. All projections clearly show that many jobs will at least, in part, be automated in the coming years

- Although unemployment levels are hitting record lows around the world, job vacancy rates have reach shockingly high proportions. The abilities of the unemployed do not match the skills required by vacant jobs, making it difficult for them to return to work

- Most economies are suffering from a talent scarcity. The same industry can be undergoing layoffs while other areas lack the qualified and competent talent required

- Technical competency and soft skills have become the most important success factors for workers today

Workers who have the highest risk of being left behind and therefore need training in this area the most, are the least likely to receive it. Company training programmes are supporting skilled workers and leaving the weakest groups alone and unprepared. This brings the potential for certain groups to suffer from high levels of chronic unemployment.

We live in interesting times. CEOs are clear on the challenge. In the 21st PwC CEO survey, 80% indicated a concern with talent availability and their feeling of accountability for reskilling current workers[27]. The war for talent has evolved to what may become devasting proportions. Coupled with the tension in economic well-being, this necessitates swift and decisive action. Action that is collaborative and coordinated; engaging governments, business, associations, unions, individuals and the community at large to engage in the solution.

Chapter 2: Challenge for Governments

This is the time for government, business and social society to work together. In this chapter, we compare the alarming skills shortage to the increase in industry demand. A disconnect that is causing the grave situation being seen in most developed countries today. We look at the challenge faced by many Ministries of Labour, Economy and Education. Searching for a balance between 'expected' curative solutions for unemployment and providing visionary leadership for upskilling that centres on that ephemeral 'future job', is not easy. Current efforts revolve around concrete and effective skills strategies that, executed correctly, will carry us forward towards meaningful and inspiring work for all. Finally, we would be remiss not to discuss the link between the widening skills gap and the potential for massive damage not just to our workforce, but to our society.

Unemployment & Job Vacancy

In May 2018, Eurostat estimated that 17.207 million men and women in the EU28 were unemployed, confirming that unemployment dropped over the last 18 years. It is now below 3% in Japan and 4% in the USA[28]. Average unemployment in the EU is hovering at 6.8% and decreasing steadily. It is easy to think that the economy is on the upswing[29], but these figures can mainly be attributed to the change in employment rate for qualified workers. Lower skilled workers are still at higher risk of unemployment.

The enormous lack of competency in some industries and business sectors and the associated lost revenue is costing up to €200,000 per vacant job per year, and €30,000 per unemployed person per year[30]. Staggering figures, if you think about the scale of unemployment in some countries. Job vacancies increased up to 2%, in some cases, between Q2 2017 and Q2 2018 due to the widening skills gap[31]. A plethora of job vacancy indicators in Q1 2018, illustrate the dilemma:

- Czechia suffered a 4.8% job vacancy rate; the highest percentage in the EU

- Job vacancies in Belgium (3.5%), Germany and Sweden (both 2.9%) are alarming compared to the 2.2% average vacant jobs in the EU

- Overall 4.5 million jobs are currently vacant in the EU. This represents approximately €450 billion of lost revenue per annum (circa 3% of the EU's GDP)

Education is a substantial influencer. Even a medium-level education is an important influence in finding a job[32]. Employment rates differ substantially according to the level of education[33]. For example, the employment rate of people aged 25 to 64 who have completed a tertiary education (short-cycle tertiary, bachelor's, master's, doctoral level or equivalents) was 84.8% across the EU-28 in 2016. This is much higher than the average rate (54.3%) for those who have a primary or lower secondary education. This low-education group, in addition to already being at high-risk for unemployment, was hardest hit by the financial crisis. The employment rate in this group fell 5.1% between 2007 and 2013, compared to 1.7% for medium-educated workers, and 1.8% for those with higher education.

NEET: Not in Employment, Education or Training

In May 2018, Eurostat estimated that youth unemployment for the EU28 stood at 15.1%, compared with 17.2% from the year before. In the Spring of 2018, the lowest rates of youth unemployment were observed in Malta (4.8%), Germany (6.1%), Estonia (6.8%) and the Netherlands (6.9%), while the highest were recorded in

Greece (43.2%), Spain (33.8%) and Italy (31.9%)[9]. Although this important youth unemployment rate is falling, they remain in the double-digits for many countries.

On average, 16.9% of youths age 20 to 24 years old are listed in the NEET category in the OECD. As well, the 34% NEET in Italy and 33% in Turkey, represent millions of youth who are already in a very difficult situation, with no skills to offer to the market. Therefore, this group especially has a high probability of poverty and unemployment in their future. Across the OECD, young people are 2.5 times more likely to be unemployed than adults over 25. During the Global Financial Crisis of 2007-2008, youth employment took a large hit and has struggled to make gains in the ensuing years. In further chapters we will talk about how automation will put many jobs at risk in the near- to mid-future, but for young people looking for employment, it will disproportionately affect less qualified workers in sectors such as retail or logistics.

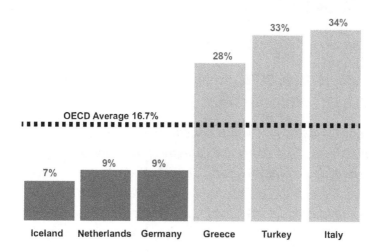

Figure #04: Lowest/Highest NEET

PwC research shows that the OECD could add around $1.2 trillion to total GDP, if countries with higher NEET rates among 20- to 24-year-olds, reduced unemployment for this sector to German levels[34]. Of course, the countries that would derive the most benefit from this would be those with the highest NEET rates. For example, if Italy could match Germany's NEET, it could see an increase of approximately 8.4% in its GDP.

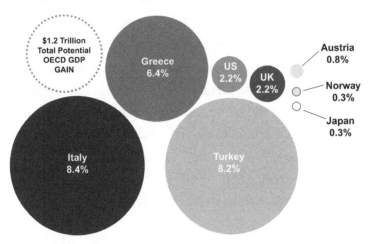

Figure #05: Potential OECD GDP Gain/Country

The president of the ECB, recently called upon governments and businesses to collaborate in addressing this important issue...

> *"Youth employment and productivity growth create a **virtuous circle**. When firms become more productive, they are more likely to employ young people. And when young people have such opportunities, they can capitalise on their skills, adding to productivity growth, which among other benefits for society will lead to higher wages. **Youth unemployment breaks this virtuous circle: it is a drag on innovation and impedes knowledge diffusion by decreasing mobility**."*
> Mario Draghi, 22nd September 2017

Millions of people in Europe and the Middle East, have already finished their formal education, but are out of work. They have little chance to reintegrate unless the entire process of knowledge and skills acquisition is reengineering to target sustainable jobs.

The Middle East: A Lost Workforce?

More 108 million (+28%) of the Middle Eastern population are between 15 and 29 years old. This is the highest number of young people to transition to adulthood in the region's history. 5- to 24-year-olds comprise approximately 20% of populations in Egypt, Iraq, Lebanon, Libya, Morocco, Oman, Sudan, Syria, Tunisia, Yemen, Jordan, Algeria, and Saudi Arabia. In Arab countries, young people are the fastest growing segment of the population. With approximately 60% under 25, this is one of the most youthful regions in the world.

Today, studies show that education systems are falling behind globally, and the UAE is no exception. The Programme for International Student Assessment (PISA) identified the UAE as having one of the most rapidly improving education systems, but also noted that in mathematics, reading and science, students still perform substantially below the average levels of achievement seen in advanced economies. In a global survey regarding young people and business, 40% of employers cited lack of skills as the main reason for entry-level job vacancies, while 60% said that new graduates were not adequately prepared for the world of work. Gaps are not just limited to technical skills and STEM subject degrees. Soft skills such as communication and effective teamwork fall within this deficit. Job market surveys and testimonials indicate that graduates today lack essential critical thinking, creativity skills and the ability to work under pressure. Designing a robust organisational structure that prepares the company for the future is a key priority for CEOs in the Middle East and around the world. Therefore, supporting the creation of a scalable and skilled workforce will be particularly important for governments.

Almost every government acknowledges that upskilling is a top priority if we are to ensure the economic health of nations and business today. Even so, the challenges associated with developing an effective upskilling strategy, have led to a void that is not easily filled. Many governments focus on short-term fixes and programmes that employ people who have been deemed unemployable, yet they do little to address fundamental issues related to skill and capability updating. These fixes may be doing more harm than good.

Some governments subsidise not-for-profits to hire and retain older or low-skilled workers who suffer from chronic unemployed. These subsidised jobs, while they decrease the percentage of unemployed in certain regions, create a skewed picture of the economy. They continue to draw from tax coffers – and will for years – robbing other sectors of funds. This issue produces a number of unintended outcomes including:

1) **prolonging unemployability**: older workers are not refreshing or learning new skills, leaving them in low-skill jobs/without meaningful employment. The hiring organisations remain focused on filling positions with obsolete skills, falling further and further behind digital times

2) **creating roadblocks**: that stop government and business from addressing the 'elephants in the room' – why organisations are permitted to layoff older, productive employees, just to reduce their bottom-line payroll and benefits costs

3) **prolonging unemployment** in the younger population. In many cases, the jobs awarded to older workers by not-for-profits, would normally be entry-level jobs for youth. The subsidy, therefore, removes avenues of gainful employment for youth

who seek their first job. This produces the knock-on effect of unemployed youth having to depend upon ageing parent for support[35]

4) **slowing government activities** that would focus on building the skill sets required to ensure future economic success and sustainable growth of the economy, as more and more funds are poured into sustaining unemployable workers[35]

These heavy investments are taking many economies in the wrong direction; creating barriers to productive action that could prepare economies for the inevitable downturn. Programmes that subsidise unemployable skills stop the population from acquiring skills they need to be hired, *and* paid, by the marketplace today. For the last ten years, many governments have put much of their effort into reducing the unemployment rate. It's time for this focus to change. Remedial job action does not spark the economy. We must enable workforce assessment and upskilling in areas that will become – or are already in the process of becoming – critical in developing sectors[36].

Main Messages

Leadership, responsibility and accountability are elements integral to the successful resolution of today's unemployment and educational challenge. Looking at the role that national leadership plays to address this issue also gives us insight into the root of present challenges and future solutions.

NEET and unemployment numbers demonstrate the increasing gap between what the education and apprenticeship systems are teaching and what the market requires. Failure to anticipate and plan, leads to an inordinate level of risk and compromises growth. A failure to anticipate education, qualification and skills requirements will endanger the sustainable development of business and cause a massive waste of human, social and financial capital that could represent several trillion euro just for Europe. Couple with this the negative impact on social cohesion and potential destabilisation of democracy caused by the rise of extremist political parties that profit from leveraging human distress and the path becomes clear.

Governments must augment their efforts with skills strategies, plans, skills banks, and other tools to ensure our students and working population have a meaningful future. Over the last five years only eleven countries have used a child to adulthood educational framework. What an opportunity for courageous and visionary political leaders to trust long-term investment in education and upskilling. This is certainly the most important societal challenge for the next 10 years. Providing the right framework to enable upskilling throughout at-risk populations, and support for economic growth, will improve social cohesion.

Chapter 3: Challenge for Corporations

In recent years, we have witnessed the drastic transformation and, in some cases, the fall of iconic companies which failed to embrace new technology. Giants like Nokia and Blackberry nearly disappeared as they struggled to embrace the smartphone wave. Even as we write this book, the retail industry is reeling as global and national brands such as Toy r'Us, H&M, and Carrefour, either close or undergo radical network restructuring. At the same time, some retail companies continue to thrive and expand. Products and pricing strategies are clear differentiators but understanding new consumer habits are becoming more critical to survival and success. The boom of online sales, the ability to offer clients new experiences via digital tools, and the power to obtain real-time analyse of customer behaviours and preferences via big data are just the tip of the iceberg.

In large companies, technology skills are clearly on the agenda. There is increasing awareness that technology is in the process of, or soon will be, disrupting business. Yet despite organisational efforts to upskill workers, there is still a long way to go before business has a clear vision of what is required, especially in sectors populated mostly by small- and medium-sized enterprises (SME). Although 67% of CEOs state that they have a responsibility to reskill their workforce, the 'people agenda' seems to be stalled, and is postponed even more in the SME sector, putting employees who work for those businesses at even more risks.

How are corporations dealing with out-dated knowledge and skills obsolescence? From the stakeholders' point of view there are a variety of factors causing competency gaps. To have any chance of success, companies must tackle the skills gap from multiple angles. Changes in business and organisational structures are caused by the quest to find the right talent that can fill the ever-increasing chasm in job vacancies. We are in a competency war.

The New War for Talent

The expression, War for Talent, was first used in 1997 to describe the increasingly competitive landscape for high-demand knowledge workers. The definition holds true today, but the root cause has changed dramatically. Shifting demographics, accelerating technology introduction, and the transformation of the world of work, are only three game-changers. Today, we find ourselves in a highly complex and rapidly evolving business environment as the war for talent accelerates.

From the construction sector, factories, professional services, to banking, the quest for competent talent is more intense than ever. Corporations spend more and more money to deploy more sophisticated tools that enable them to source, attract, test and retain talent. There is a boom in the global market for HR-related software and technology. From the ERP-type suites, to the thousands of very specific products using AI, RPA, chatbots, big data, or often a combination of these technologies. The appetite for HR tech seems insatiable. We see this high value reflected in the market and in the eagerness of Venture Capitalists to invest in this type of HR tech company today.

Unrealised Potential

A recent study by the Korn Ferry Institute, calculated that by 2030, we will be able to attribute $8.5 trillion in unrealised revenue to talent shortages[37]. This represents $162 billion just in the US. It's feasible, looking at the projections, that India, one of few resource exporters by then, could overtake the USA as the world's top tech giant. By 2030, China too, will face a talent shortage of 12 million workers or more, while Japan may struggle to find the 18 million workers it needs to keep its economy afloat. Organisations must make talent strategies a key priority and take steps now to educate, train and upskill their existing workforces. In terms of lifelong learning, Jean-Marc Laouchez, president of the Korn Ferry Institute, says, "Constant learning – driven by both workers and organisations – will be central to the future of work, extending far beyond the traditional definition of learning and development."

Is this just an isolated study? The Manpower Employment Outlook Survey assesses the current situation. According to this study, talent shortages since 2006 have reached a record high, with a global 'difficulty to hire average' standing at 45% in the 43 countries surveyed. Fuelled by a lack of labour, ageing demographics, and immigration restrictions, it reached a record 89% in Japan in 2016.

Interestingly, we see that the larger the company, the more challenging hiring becomes. Higher wage demands, and more diversified jobs offered by smaller players are tough hurdles to overcome when nearly a third of these employers cite the lack of applicants as their main reason for job vacancies[38]. In fact, in October 2018, the Wall Street Journal reported that wages and salaries paid to private-sector employees in the United States increased 3.1% from Q3 2017. That was strongest year-over-year gain since the second quarter of 2008. Even worse, 20% cite the lack of appropriate experience and 27%, the applicants' lack of either hard skills or the soft skills needed to get the job done.

For HR directors too, talent is a top agenda item. While most companies have, or are finalising, their digital plan for hardware, systems and process management tools, many are still struggling to understand the widespread consequences of digital automation on their people. We see a growing concern about the impact of frequent and simultaneous introductions of a plethora of new technologies to the workforce. Classic tools such as workforce planning hardly give answers to these concerns or other critical questions.

HR directors and departments who are not able or willing to keep up with the evolution of technology and digitalisation of the workplace are in jeopardy. The depth of the problem is clear. Organisations face important challenges regarding upskilling workers. Prevalent factors influencing workforce skills requirements include:

- new technology introduction, Industry 4.0, and the Global Value Chain phenomenon

- the shrinking talent pool and skills gap in current workforces caused by companies investing in 'non-targeted maintenance training' instead of targeted upskilling

- stronger border policies and migration restrictions

- the dilemma of multi-generational workforces, expectations, priorities, values and new ways of working for corporations and their employees as the retirement age slowly moves towards 70 in most EU countries

- recurring issues with lack of innovation and creative thinking caused by insufficient attention to the untapped talent pool, diversity and gender equality

Industry 4.0: No People, No Transformation

Looking at the Industry 4.0 wave in manufacturing adds a unique lens to the perspective. Industry 3.0 automated single machines and processes. Industry 4.0 encompasses end-to-end digitisation and data integration throughout the whole value chain. An interesting example of the Industry 4.0 challenge is a client who is currently transforming their end-to-end moulding production process. Order to delivery takes about 60 days but their 'factory of the future' ambition is to reduce that time to six days. This obviously, goes hand-in-hand with a sharp transformation of the workforce. Companies moving to the Industry 4.0 model can:

- offer digital products and services; building partnerships and optimising customer-facing activities

- operate connected physical and virtual assets; transforming and integrating all operations and internal activity

With only 10% of global manufacturing companies championing Industry 4.0 and two-thirds just beginning the journey, **millions** of industrial jobs will be transformed in the years to come. Yet, according to the study, two-thirds of companies lack a human resources transformation vision. This is confirmed by another study performed in Luxembourg (2017), which indicated that 90% of companies had not anticipated the consequences of technology on their human resources systems and processes[39]. The Global Digital Operations Study highlights eight key findings; it's no surprise that one of them is that people are central to digital transformation; no people, no transformation[40]. There are four key elements used by digital champions to successfully evolve their culture and to shape the HR management eco-system:

Skills: workers exhibit diverse skills. They work in agile ways. Organisations show strong capabilities in data analytics, human-machine interaction and technology-supported decision-making.

Mind-set and behaviour: openness to technology, acceptance of failure, creativity, innovation, general curiosity, rapid decision-making and a non-hierarchical 'best idea counts' mentality is key to a digital culture.

Organisation: internally and externally integrated cross-functional teams, on-demand labour from network platforms and talent pools. Using hackathons, accelerators, digital agencies, research institutes and universities builds a flexible, hybrid organisation. The brand is associated with digital and enables recruitment. Finally, co-development projects with technical schools and universities are the norm and are used to access and onboard workers with the right skills.

Career development: innovative and smart digital ideas are stimulated by real-time feedback paired with frequent formal appraisals, incentives and compensation schemes. Flexible work and telecommuting are paired with free-time aimed at encouraging continuous improvement in company operations.

With only 10% of industrial companies having developed this people-centric eco-system, most remain in an analogue culture, struggling to evolve towards a digital framework. The main differences between the two cultures are the way decisions are made, innovation blossoms, and teams are organised and collaborate. In that survey, 59% of digital champions have invested heavily in training to upgrade staff, 52% have flat hierarchies, quick decision-making and regard failure as an accepted part of the development process.

Global Value Chain Evolution

The analysis of the Global Value Chain described in the 2018 OECD report[41] complements this investigation into corporate and manufacturing challenges. Over the last decades, the way we produce goods has changed. Many regions or countries have specialised in fabricating semi-finished products and/or specific components in the Global Value Chain (GVC). Today, most products are assembled using components coming from all over the world.

Obviously, this is a highly competitive market and countries are competing intensely to enter, remain in it, or to move up the value chain; decreasing their dependence on others. According to

OECD figures, 30% of jobs in business were sustained by consumers in foreign markets. This number rises to over 50% in some small European countries. Here, skills play a key role in reducing workers' exposure to the risk of offshoring. By 2025 most companies will review their production facilities and relocate to locations that provide the appropriate workforce and market. This highlights the importance of fit in terms of specific types of jobs. When the job involves face-to-face interaction, the need to be on-site, or decision-making, it is less likely to be off-shored. Ensuring that workers have the correct skills, enables them to adapt their jobs to fluctuating needs more fluidly. The study emphasises that workers' cognitive skill and readiness to learn, play a fundamental role in international integration. There also seems to be a clear link between the level of exports and workers' cognitive skills level.

The Heckscher-Ohlin model of international trade, and a variety of empirical studies, demonstrate that a more skilled workforce enables a country to specialise in high-skilled activities[42]. This seems logical as skills enable workers to assimilate new technologies; to adapt and improve quality. Skills not only circulate throughout the firm but also to the rest of economy[43]. To reap the full benefits of new technology and to address the challenge of production fragmentation, we must invest in skills at the country *and* corporate levels. For firms, the studies evidence a link between better management policies and the level of education of both managers and non-managers. Developing a mix of skills, including entrepreneurial and management skills, is important to success.

Lack of Training Investment

Another way to look at the skills gap is by analysing training undertaken by individuals after completing their 'formal education'. According to Eurostat, 10.8% of the adult population in the EU participated in lifelong learning (% of population aged 24 to 64) in

2016. We see major differences between Nordic countries, where 25% to 30% of the adult population engage in this type of learning, compared to quite a wide dispersal in all other countries[44]. Sadly, these numbers indicate an ineffective learning strategy that is not enough to meet and overcome the challenges we face.

According to Statista, the amount of training received by employees annually in the US varied from 42.2 to 54.3 hours, depending of the size of the company[45]. This is four times France's average of 12.7 hours per year per worker and 43.5% of workers have access to continuous in-house training (2008)[46]. Interestingly, half of respondents reported that on-the-job training is the most common. According to CVTS 3 and 4 surveys in France, 76% of workers had access to in-house training in 2010 and 47% acquiring competencies[47]. Only 42% of the training taken focused on (or had as a main objective) to develop flexibility, ability to multitask and/or to build other soft skill competencies. Digging even further, only 15% were focused on an activity change such as developing skills for a change in job or to avoid the loss of a job, but this category of training was 81% effective!

In 2015, 23% of UK organisations provided employees with an average of 40 hours of training, but 40% of companies surveyed gave less than 20 hours of training during the same year. Although five to six days of training per year is already much better than the norm, it is not enough to meet the learning challenges we face today. It is even more interesting to understand the type of training that workers attend. In Luxembourg, the average IT training last five hours, job on-boarding 37 hours, and language training 11 hours. This indicates that the focus is not really to ensure the development of future technical or required soft skills[48].

Generally, training investments aim at ensuring that the employee is more comfortable in the current job (49%), or to comply with new regulatory issues (31%). Only 15% focus on protecting against job obsolescence or on learning skills required to obtain new employment. Interestingly, the efficiency and effectiveness for the first two objectives reached 94% and 98% effectiveness, compared with 81% for the latter. These shocking numbers indicate that out of an average of five training days, companies spend merely 1 day on future competencies that either protect the employee from losing their job or allow them to acquire new employment. One could argue about absolute figures, but the distribution by training subjects is quite inadequate.

Tech Acceleration Impacts Training Outlook

Often, corporate training focuses on the very short-term (technical training) or the very long-term (managerial training). This focus leads to a misalignment and disconnect from the accelerating tech waves that are narrowing substantially the lag between decision-making and real implementation. Companies which previously had a rather long runway between the decision to invest in new tech or factories and the actual implementation or opening, are now working on an abbreviated schedule.

Accelerating implementation is also coupled with more rapid obsolescence. Through the evolution of implementation methodologies, we see that even new technology itself is becoming obsolete more quickly. Agile's minimum viable product (MVP) methodology, the boom in artificial intelligence (AI), and related software, have accelerated the speed of technology introduction. Kay Kurzweil's words are a stark illustration of the changes we have witnessed in the last few decades.

> "The first computers were designed on paper and assembled by hand. Today, they are designed on computer workstations with the computers themselves working out many details of the next generation's de-

sign and are then produced in fully automated factories with only limited human intervention."[49]

But for many companies and workers the reality that we are experiencing today is still just a pulse of things to come. The challenge for most companies then, is to ensure that they have a keen eye on the horizon with a 'future focus' context for all training.

Lack of People, or Lack of Skills?

Although unemployment rates in most countries are currently at their lowest since 2007, the skills being taught to, and mastered by, unemployed workers do not match the current demand. 73% of employers surveyed for the 2018 Hays US Salary Guide indicated that lack of available training and development, and fewer people entering the industry, are the main cause for their skills shortage[50]. The Manpower Group's Employment Outlook Survey underscores this trend, projecting a lack of 85.2 million workers and $8.5 trillion in unrealised revenue[51]. The only country that seems to be winning the War for Talent is India. All other economies have strong talent deficits, including China, which will swing from a talent surplus in 2020 to a 12 million worker deficit by 2030.

Mid-skilled jobs represent 40% of all employment across the OECD and demand in this area is growing. Interestingly, the ten most in-demand jobs only require post-secondary training, not even a full university degree. Similarly, in digital jobs, college degrees are not paramount. When it comes to employability, organisations rely heavily on continuous training, since most traditional jobs in tech and digital endlessly evolve. We can learn much from this sector where the virtual circle of new technology enhancement is followed quickly by regular technology skills upgrade and/or training.

The problem with the STEM sector is not necessarily that it lacks adequate focus on training. It just does not have enough recruits coming into these professional fields to fill openings. Technology, media, and telecoms (TMT) are projected to suffer a shortage of 4.3 million workers by 2030, and $450 billion in lost revenues. Here, the most acute shortage is forecast to be in the US. Where, along with the UK, it is projected to lose $162 billion in revenue by 2030 and to suffer from a shortage of 600,000 workers. The hardest hit of all will be Hong Kong and Singapore. All the signs point to a tech talent shortage in Singapore. Although Singapore universities are producing around 400 tech graduates a year, the demand is around a 1,000. This would put Singapore's ambition to be a leader in the FinTech industry in jeopardy. Indeed, deficits of highly skilled workers in those two countries will reach a record 80% for Hong Kong and 61% for Singapore. Here again, the up-skilling of existing workforces will be key to maintain competitive-ness[51].

Japan will also lose 300,000 workers a year and is forecast to be 18 million workers short by 2030; threatening Japan's position in the world's top five tech markets[53]. Even as Japan tries to partially solve its talent shortage with extensive use of technologies in various sectors, that strategy could be at risk due to a lack of resources. 40% of companies there are currently facing difficultly hiring tech specialists. Europe is showing the same pattern, with a shortage of 500,000 ICT professionals forecast for 2020. The digital skills gap continues to grow in Europe, putting jobs and economic health at risk.

For India, predictions are more positive. It will have a record surplus of workers by 2030. With its strong supply of skilled resources in Technology, Media and Telecoms (TMT), Bangalore could surpass USA tech hubs before 2030.

Looking across sectors, over 10 million jobs will suffer from labour/

skills shortages in financial and business service sectors, with massive shortages of workers in the USA. As well, financial centres in the USA, UK, Singapore and Hong Kong will likely experience a combined 2.6 million worker deficit. Industry has the same pattern. By 2030, Japan, currently third in global manufacturing, will fail to generate even $194 billion in revenue, and Germany only $77 billion, due to talent shortages. Small economies are also victims of this phenomenon, most likely because their main resource is people, and opportunities to grow are tightly aligned with the level of skills in the population. So, it is clear. There is a War for Talent. It is here to stay ... and is even predicted to swell as time progresses.

The HR Tech Boom

Yesterday, corporations paid little attention to HR and their tools. The focus was on finance and other 'productive functions'. But corporations have evolved. Management understands the critical nature of HR, without which, no sales, production, or research can take place. HR is hyped regularly in the media and in the tech development world these days. From a rather poor offering, mainly focus on the 'must haves' such as payroll, or HR ERP (Enterprise Resources Planning) systems operating key HR processes such as recruitment, performance management, or training, we see a real explosion. The list of available HR IT software applications is almost infinite, but many have focused solely on recruitment, talent management, and learning. Now, HR's toolbox is being enriched to deal with the myriad of personnel management and development requirements.

The use of big data and AI enables organisations to spot talent it might otherwise miss, predict attrition, and even potentially forecast the performance of newcomers in a given environment or situation. The HR technology market is being flooded by suppliers, intent on providing digital solutions for sourcing, hiring, retaining, and developing employees. The HR Tech world has been booming for a while. We are far from the greyish HR world of the 90s.

This new HRIS world is active and engaged. As human resource management becomes an even more influential key success factor for companies, the actors are more visible and are gaining traction. Technology is a key success factor for this critical area. Are HR personnel keeping up with these developments? Just as organisations must find the correct mix of upskilling opportunities for their workers, HR professionals must ensure that their skills are keeping pace with rapid technical developments in their field.

For example, software which organises the recruitment process saves huge amounts of time; tracking applicants and ensuring all relevant parties are involved. These systems have advanced to the point where they can now store information from the candidate's application to contract production. The system can even store and analyse opinions from interviews to ensure that final decisions are effective and unbiased.

But many questions remain: How to find applicants? How to test their soft and hard skills? How to make sure personalities are aligned with corporate culture or that resumes are accurate and truthful? Yesterday, it was possible to address all these questions using two essentials; time and money... but if money remains a constraint, time is the real challenge. Today, companies can receive hundreds, if not thousands of applications for a single job. How might a company deal with such high volume, especially knowing that social media is observing its behaviours, and pointing out all perceived conduct flaws?

Today, corporations have no other choice but to adopt technology. Companies must execute HR processes, while being observed, scrutinised, and rated on social media ... in real time. They must be able to track what they are doing with applications, provide evidence that they treat applicants with fairness, and confirm that they respect diversity in their workforce. This all must be done quickly enough to beat the competition in hiring the best candidates. New HR tools support the execution of these large-scale activities economically, and with reasonable speed. Thanks to digitalisation, some tools can even, to a certain degree, incorporate company policies and values, so that applicants can be ranked to find the best match for the culture.

HR ERP systems offer new functionality to balance and accelerate the recruitment process. More importantly, hundreds of products are now available to support the recruiter: sourcing tools use algorithms to spot workers' behaviours on social media and predict their 'readiness to move', recruitment chatbots engage with potential applicants and ask the first set of questions to qualify applicants. These tools adapt to applicants' schedules more effectively than the human recruiter.

Tools that test for soft and hard skills, learning ability, IT literacy, specific software mastery, resume accuracy, etc. remove the rote work that would take a single individual many hours, or even days, to complete. Obviously, the company equipped with the right tools is able to source better candidates and be more accurate in its selection process than its competitor. It can provide the new-joiner a smooth and faster orientation and integration experience, through digitalisation and automated processes. Highly sophisticated on-boarding tools enable newcomers to become as effective as possible, as soon as possible, and track their journey through the first months of employment with their company.

In 2017, there were more than 600 HR tech start-ups in Paris alone[54]. Popular sector conventions, such as the HRD (Human Resources Director Magazine), HR Tech Summits in Singapore,

Toronto and Sydney, or Unleash in Las Vegas, London and Amsterdam, gather thousands of HRIS professionals to hear famous speakers like Richard Branson. Several times a year, leading ERP vendors such as Workday and SuccessFactors, gather thousands of client users and prospects to locations around the world; showcasing their new functionalities. Integrators and eco-system partners pay large sums to be visible and demonstrate to clients the breadth of both their applications and the extensive software eco-system they offer with their partners (a bit like an App Store). Myriads of start-ups attending these conventions, develop application programming interfaces (API's) in order to integrate smoothly and ease their sales process. HR tech is big business.

Observers can also spot this on the VC and M&A markets. In the past two years, venture capital and private equity investors have poured close to $2 billion into this market, with more than $900 million invested in the first seven months of 2017. Fundraising for HR start-ups has never been so important. CB Insights quoted a 2016 record of approximately 402 deals worth $2.2 billion. The internet shows M&A activity for some of the most important players in the HR-Tech field is growing[55]. It illustrates the dynamism in that market.

2018 saw one of the largest HR tech acquisitions. Recruit (owner of Indeed.com) announced the $1.2 billion acquisition of Glassdoor, the popular company/jobs review site. While earlier in 2018, ADP acquired Workmarket, a software solution that enables the freelance economy for companies such as Yahoo and The New York Times. Staffing agency Adecco paid over $400 million for the popular technology training academy General Assembly. In early June, Workday announced its first HR acquisition for 2018; Rallyteam, an internal mobility solution.

But who is using all of these tools? Who are the clients for all these systems and applications? It's no surprise that many of these start-ups have prestigious clients that are listed on the New York Stock Exchange (NYSE), or are part of the Fortune 100. These star corporations are testing innovative tools, on a limited use-case basis, in their own innovation labs. Accurately evaluating the concepts and software using agile principles, they verify the ROI, corporate fit and efficiency of potential solutions, before regional or global deployment for the winners. They are in a quest for speed and efficiency; delivering value at the fastest pace possible, for less money.

Training & Development via Tech

Learning and Development is another market going digital. We briefly touched on the process, but let's look at content and delivery. These days, classic classroom training is in heavy competition with a variety of digital tools that enable participants to be remotely trained and tested on almost any topic, at their convenience. We won't go into how e-learning or massive open online learning (MOOCs) developed over recent years or list the huge investment leading training editors are making in digitise content. The most interesting element is the enormous effort IT players are making. CISCO, Google and Microsoft understand the need to offer convenient training. For years, they have invested substantial funds to build IT curriculum that enables people to train on their tools. As technology development and evolution moves at a faster and faster pace, so does the need to learn it.

Educational resources are scarce, so digital training tools provide quality training, anywhere, anytime. These training modalities offer more than just a way to train workers on the newest tech development, they are marketing tools and image building vehicles. For major brands, they are big money-makers with huge market valuation. For the individual, digital learning and development platforms provide customised learning paths, allowing them to position themselves effectively in the IT job jungle. For example, people who aspire to an IT career and want to ensure their skills continue to be current, can access the IDC Hot Jobs Index that is linked to the Cisco Learning Network. It provides an excellent overview of existing in-demand job skills. It also, more importantly, highlights future requirements.

In 2017, Cisco's technical training was available in 21 countries and had a revenue of €8 million. By 2025, the revenue from this stream is projected to top €1 billion. This indicates that certification is becoming even more valuable to workers that many types of diplomas and degrees. As French Labour Minister, Murielle Pénicaud, said just before the vote for the new vocational training law, "the best protection … for your professional life are competencies." (Le Figaro 1 Aug 2018)

The Multi-generation Workforce Dilemma

Today, the landscape of professional life is changing. Companies might have up to four different generations working under the same roof. Millennials (Gen Y, born 1981-1996) who are very recent entrants into the job market, work alongside baby boomers (born 1946-1964) who are already starting to retire and exit the workforce. Behaviours, ways of working and thinking, and even values and priorities are diverging. This tension between work generations translates into a change in the routine of an organisation and influences expectations and perspectives. Companies must be able to manage all the elements associated with a multi-generational workforce and still do business.

Workers from different generations may need different stimuli to feel their career is fulfilling. Simple elements such as the need for recognition, flexibility and autonomy (Gen Ys), can cause challenges within teams. A hallmark of Millennials is their thirst for promotion, experience and higher wages. They want challenge, learning, autonomy, connection; valuing meeting people (and clients), networking, and travel. Gen Ys might even ask for internal, international, CSR assignments, or to run a major project just a few months after they join. They wish to receive direct and frequent feedback about their performance, to understand the main purpose of their job, and how it aligns and supports company goals. This means that a Millennial will join a company and leave in nine months if they don't feel connected and part of the team. Many baby boomers with their strong sense of hierarchy, loyalty, discipline, and work ethic, find this unacceptable behaviour.

Younger workers are passionate about finding better work-life balance. Gen Xs find it normal for both men and women to take parental leave. One of the indicators is the growing trend in the West for fathers to become primary care-givers, or to at least take on a more active role in child-rearing. This balances the load between partners and provides a more stable and positive home-life. It is also causing a sharp increase in parental leave for men, where that option exists. In many cases, this choice would be an exception to the rule for more senior workers.

Baby boomers put aside their private lives and values almost completely when they made up the largest portion of the working population, during their formative work years. The pendulum has swung full arc and new generations are much less willing to give up their private time and personal goals. They seek social benefits *and* responsibility.

An important aspect of this change in attitude that is not getting much attention, is the younger generation's increased focus on corporate values, behaviours, and social responsibility. Expectations towards employers have changed. For the younger generations, challenge and purpose must align with their ethics. They thirst to know and understand the corporation's true spirit; the values that are lived, not just espoused, and today, it is quite easy to ascertain if a company walks its own talk. Thanks to the boom in social media, this information is ubiquitous, readily available, and immediate. People have access to so much information that they sometimes know more about the company (news, moves, incidents) than many middle or top managers. Employees do not look at their employer the same way as even ten years ago. Their focus is on more than just their pay-check and that is changing the talent market and corporations.

Changes to HR policies, work distribution, office design and job configuration are responses to this interesting mix of inter-generational challenges. The era of individual and closed offices is nearly over. Open-plan workspaces, co-working or even shared desk environments are becoming the norm. These new workspace configurations lower facility expenses and aim to boost interaction in hopes of increasing innovation by leveraging diversity. Companies are also slowly tackling the standard hierarchical model and becoming flatter. In some cases, people no longer report to a manager, but instead move from project to project, depending on their availability and skills. This new way of working also requires people to play by new rules. They must seek feedback proactively and take responsibility for upgrading their own skills to ensure they stay in high demand. This new model of higher independence and also more responsibility may not fit all workers. Some may require more support.

In these more challenging environments, organisations must implement intelligent strategies to attract and retain workers with the appropriate competencies. Workers' higher expectations and the shift towards following personal values, are more apt to come into play when choosing between potential employers. Enhanced learning opportunities and collaborative, lower stress workplaces can be a drawing card. Training methods as well, must respond to these varied groups. With 25% of Gen Xs (born 1965-1980) choosing online training, compared to 13% of Gen Z (post-millennials, born 1997-present), the data can be counter-intuitive. A deeper dive into 'generational characteristics' using multiple surveys, shows that loneliness is endemic for Gen Zs. A recent survey conducted by Cigna found that in the US, Gen Zs and Millennials are the loneliest groups in the workplace[56]. It's no surprise that Gen Zs favour more classroom training. Gen Xs, being more independent and cynical, fall somewhere between, which can be quite a challenge for managers. Matching the different learning pattern and meeting expectations of specific generations can enhance and enrich the workplace. The challenge is organising proper developmental opportunities in the context of these new ways of working.

Communication behaviours also vary radically. Millennials sitting in the same open-plan office will use instant messaging, while baby boomers prefer in-person conversations. This diversity has far-reaching consequences in work organisation and scheduling, including workers taking longer unpaid personal or parental leave.

Remote working had almost insurmountable barriers less than a decade ago. With the advent of ubiquitous residential WIFI, affordable home computers, video conference commoditisation and a much more competitive communication network, remote working is a basic fixture for most organisations. Many companies have remote work policies enabling work from remote-satellite offices, co-working spaces, or home. Today, the market is exploding with remote monitoring software that provides real-time data about work habits and how work is completed. Every organisation has a variety of choices in terms of specific software to enable and monitor remote workers, and to identify potential skills development opportunities.

Diversity: Higher Revenue, Better Results

We've heard the statistics about diversity for quite a while and it translates into some impressive figures. In 2015, McKinsey published <u>The Power of Parity</u> Report[56]. It and many similar reports confirm that diversity leads to higher profitability. Advancing diversity and women's equality could add $12 trillion to global growth by 2025. Using a 'full potential' labour market scenario, where women have the same opportunities and identical roles as men, that figure jumps even higher to $28 trillion; 26% of GDP for 2025! In a business environment suffering from an accelerating 'war for talent' we cannot rule out the value of diversity. There is ample evidence that it is possible to realise the potential GDP gains indicated in the report. Let's look at just a few figures to make it clear.

- 49.5% of today's global population is female, but they make up only 40% of world's workforce[57]

- Women only hold 14.2% of the top five leadership positions in the S&P 500 and only 5% of global CEO positions

- 20% of women work in family businesses; they say that they don't have the same chance to succeed as men[58]

- A recent study of 300 USA start-up investments backed by venture capitalists showed that companies founded by females performed 63% better than ones with an all-male founding team

- A study of over 90,000 companies in 35 countries, performed by Lehigh University, demonstrated a clear link between female representation on the Board and market performance

- Only 35% of female Millennials believe they can rise to senior positions[59]

- Women only hold 19% of tech-related jobs in the top 10 global tech companies[60]

- The average wage gap between men and women reached 19.1% in EU countries, 13.9% for OECD countries, 18.2% for the USA, and a shocking 34.6% in Korea

Insufficient attention on diversity, and gender in particular, causes recurring issues such as lack of innovation and creative thinking. It abandons an untapped talent pool, which is reckless human capital management. Talent pools in the West are becoming more homogeneous and smaller over time. Indeed, in Europe, women represent only 42.2% of STEM graduates (2015) but this percentage is almost 50/50 in India[61]. Sadly, in the USA this figure only hovers around the mid-30% with an outrageously low 2.9% of black and 3.6% of Latina women obtaining STEM degrees. It's no surprise that women represent only 25.5% of computer and mathematical occupations in the USA with Black, Latinas and Asian together representing as little as 10% of that population, when they comprise 38.3% of American females.

Considering this against the wave of new ways of working, multi-generation presence under the same roof, and career extension, we see HR's challenge clearly. The Future Work Skills 2020 describes the issues well:

1. **Extreme longevity**: increasing global lifespans change the nature of careers and learning

2. **Rise of smart machines**: workplace automation nudges human workers out of rote, repetitive tasks

3. **Computational world**: massive increases in sensors and processing power make the world a programmable system

4. **New media ecology**: New communication tools require new media literacy beyond text

5. **Super-structured organisations**: social technologies drive new forms of production and value creation

6. **Globally connected world**: Increased global interconnectivity puts diversity and adaptability at the centre of organisational operations[62]

Of course, diversity is not just about gender. Culture, race, age, sexual orientation, and disability are just a few categories that describe people who cannot find their place or thrive in many workplace environments. Some companies understand that diversity is critical to finding the best resources, and for producing creative and high-quality performance. In their 2017 article for Harvard Business Review, Robert D. Austin and Gary P. Pisano describe companies that are realising benefits from neurodiversity[63]. SAP is achieving quantifiable and qualitative gains in areas such as employee engagement, productivity, improvements in quality and increased capabilities in innovation. Top business schools such as INSEAD, Harvard and Yale, are capitalising on this new awareness by offering gender diversity programmes and introducing diversity awareness initiatives to attract and retain a wider variety of students. Business can no longer ignore the potential innovation and productivity gains created by a diverse workplace. Upskilling is one way to rapidly add to the diversity within an organisation or institution.

Main Messages

The world of work is evolving; people are not working for the same reasons and do not seek the same relationship that previous generations had with their employers. New 'ways of working', Industry 4.0, multi-generational workforces, diversity, and career extension are just a few of the challenges faced today. The unpredictable mix of generations can make delivery a challenge. Companies must shift their thinking about resources and be ready to optimise value from diverse staff working side by side. Some have clearly understood this and are making changes. In 2018, Disney announced a $50 million USD fund to train its employees. But few corporations are proactively dealing with this challenge. The war for talent is stronger than ever. Corporations must be willing and able to compete.

What few are discussing is the imperative to upskill HR teams to ensure they understand technologies that will impact their employee population. We are in the Industry 4.0 revolution, but we need HR 5.0 to guide policy, processes and to set standards that will ensure viable and sustainable jobs for the future. Some of HR's greatest challenges today include fostering the evolution of competencies that will allow workers to remain employable and efficient. This entails more targeted training investments and keeping a keen eye on the jobs of the future.

Chapter 4: Challenge for Workers

The shifting attitude toward work, and the longevity of positions is disrupting and transforming the labour market. We know that there is a disconnect between our traditional model of work and what younger workers expect. With the passing of the 'job for life' era, the illusion that the company is the employee's sole care-taker has been dispelled. Today the way employees approach work is also clearly changing. No longer content to perform the same job, or task, for the same employer for years, young work-ers aim for a higher autonomy over their career and shorter-term activities; workers are refusing to permanently link their future to their current employer. Instead they sell their knowledge and skill as freelancers or change jobs and employers more often. This chapter looks at the changing world of work from the employees' perspective.

Freelance and Part-time Work

The notion of 'worker' has evolved. In the past, freelancers made up a tiny portion of the working population. This mode of work was sometimes by choice, but more often by necessity, because people could not find permanent or traditional employment. Today, surveys show that freelancers currently represent up to 30% of USA workers and this percentage will only grow in the future. In 2017, Forbes predicted that 50.9% of American workers would be freelancers by 2027[64]. These important trends substantiate the forecast that there will be more freelancers than 'traditional' workers by then. According to Upwork's, 5th Annual <u>Freelancing in America Report</u>, in the USA alone, 47% of millennials, approx-imately 36% of that segment of the workforce, are freelancers[65]. These workers are increasingly freelance by choice (63%) and, on average, work for 4.5 different clients per month. The 'typical relationship' between corporations and workers today could soon be drastically redefined, as 69% of the freelancers surveyed agree that this mode of work is now perceived in a more positive light, and therefore, a more viable career option.

Is this trend similar in Europe? The figures seem to match the trends we describe above; of 184.4 million employees, 32.7 million are self-employed, and 45.3 million are part-time. The European Commission's 2016 Future of Work study indicates that the number of self-employed workers already stands at 16.4% of the labour market. That is a substantial gain from the 10.1% in 2005 and 15.8% in 2014[66]. The Centre for Research on Self-employment's (CRSE) global workshop on Freelancing & Self-employment (2018), found 15% of the active working population in the UK was self-employed in 2015[67].

Part-time workers are another aspect of today's workforce. According to Statista, the percentage of part-time worker in the USA fluctuated between 26% in 2017 and 28% in 2018. For Japan, part-time workers represent around 10% of the workforce. European part-time numbers (18.9% average) are higher, with 31.4% of female and 8.2% of male workers in 2016, although there are huge differences between countries. The percentage of part-time workers in the Netherlands stand at 46.6%, while in Hungary they make up only about 5% of the workforce[68]. These statistics indicate serious challenges for organisations and employees alike. As companies struggle to procure the skills needed for their business, it might appear that workers today are in a dominant position, but is that really the case? If we connect this mode of work with our investigation of the new reality in training, it becomes really interesting.

The question of investment in training for freelancers and part-time workers is clearly a difficult one both for the client/employer and the worker. In a world where resources are already scarce, how do these millions of workers prepare for the future? This segment of the workforce relies on their competencies and reputation to stay employed. They invest much more time to keep their skills and knowledge up-to-date taking almost double the standard training time of most workers.

According to the survey, 55% of freelancers participated in skill-related education, compared to only 30% of non-freelancers in the same 6-month period. No matter what field they are in, freelancers and independent workers must individually determine which training programme makes the most sense for their field, budget and learning needs. They must investigate and decide upon training providers and fund it personally. One might attribute this dedication to their permanent 'burning platform' of needing to remain competitive to be employable. Most freelancers manage regular learning programmes that encompass as much, if not more than their full-time counterparts. Were they to drop their learning agenda, they would most likely see a quick and direct reflection in their billable hours; with either a decrease in client engagements or a reduction in fees. So, they are quite motivated to remain trained to the highest possible level.

Freelancers seem to be acutely aware of the potential impact of digitisation. 77% of survey respondents believe that part of their work will be performed by robots or machines within 20 years, compared to 62% of non-freelancers. Looking to the immediate future, 49% agree that their work is already affected by automation/robots compared with a mere 18% of non-freelancers. How are independent workers facing this new norm? Their need to thoughtfully approach their skills development and maintenance may become even more critical. Are they willing and able to learn at the required pace? Do they have enough incentive to take on the added challenge of upskilling? What new techniques or methods allow them to learn most effectively? Where will workers who are motived to upskill find the time and the money to participate? These are just a few of the questions they face.

Burning Platforms: The Workforce Perspective

Today, we have millions of workers whose routine jobs will soon be automated. What can these individuals do? Is the worker even aware of what is coming? According to a recent PwC survey[69], 74% of interviewed workers, rather than relying on any employer, believe it is their own responsibility to update their skills. This statistic indicates that workers no longer trust their companies to actively assist them in updating their skills. Does this statistic correlate with workers' reluctance to view themselves as traditional employees in the classic organisation structure? A structure that has already failed them; in many cases, laying off staff instead of assisting them to maintain their skills.

Generally, workers are much more informed. Many people in the workforce today either have colleagues/relatives/friends living this 'downsizing/automation' situation or hear about 'worst-case scenarios' via the media. Companies using technology as the rationale for massive layoffs, see an almost immediate response to their announcement; demonised by the media and social networks. Nordea, ING and the Japanese banking industry are a few examples but there are similar cases from almost every business sector we explored.

- Nordea to Cut 'at Least' 6,000 Jobs in Fight to Stay Competitive[70] was only one headline in information that plastered media[71]. Stock prices fell, as Nordea became Bloomberg's worst performer for European financial stocks for that day [72]

- Reuter's article, ING plans to cut 7,000 job, spend on digital draws union ire[73], also highlighted the union's disapproval of the company's tactics

- Yet another example is Finextra's posting, <u>Japan's banks plan 33,000 job cuts in digital downsizing</u>[74].

Even with tech-heavy organisations, headlines about layoffs provide a unique perspective into the psyche of impacted staff.

- <u>They're liquidating us: AT&T continues layoffs and outsourcing despite profits</u>, screams the Guardian headline posted on August 28, 2018[75]

- <u>New York Daily News Layoffs Ax Half the Newsroom Staff</u>[76] was one of the headlines by the Huffington Post, on July 23, 2018. Following a 50% downsizing of the editorial staff, many took to social media to vent their frustration by lamenting the demise of journalism. Some social media posts collected hundreds of comments and were retweeted and 'liked' thousands of times[77]

Workers can easily see first-hand how organisations behave, and how their colleagues are treated when other parts of the organisation are automated. This has a tremendous impact on employee trust and engagement, not to speak of the employer's image and future capacity to recruit.

In many organisations there is a secondary outcome; the most talented workers – those who will find it easiest to obtain employment somewhere else – will jump ship more quickly, leaving critical holes in the organisation. As companies compete for fewer and fewer high-skilled workers, and positions in the job market continue to evolve, which company will candidates gravitate toward? The one that supports their employability, and trains them up to be ready for the next job, or the one undertaking massive layoffs?

Previously, we highlighted that the time allocated to training in the USA is around five days per year, in the best of cases. But this shockingly low average conceals even more unacceptable numbers. HRProfessional reports that organisations with less than 100 employees provided 12 minutes of training every six months[78]. Those statistics are evolving, as indicated in the 2017 Training Industry Report that notes a 32.5% increase in training expenditures in the USA. We can assume that this sharp increase in budget is, at least in part, a clear reaction to today's employee recruitment and training challenge. Although budgets are increasing, the figures clearly indicate the challenge workers face to keep up to date with their competencies[79].

In general, there is still a large gap between the time and budget that organisations allocate to training and what is needed. As always, it comes back to the classic dilemma between short-term profit, production and investment in the future. For now, let's consider the worker who receives an average of five days training per year. How do they react? Are they looking for online training/ MOOCs, independent evening classes, or do they expect their employer to anticipate and address all their training needs? To examine these questions more fully, we must consider the different types of workers.

Of course, there can be a wide variation in training and attitudes depending upon the industry or size of company. Large organisations and tech companies are known to pay considerable attention to this very important aspect of their competitive edge.

SMEs, on the other hand, do not always have the latitude or funds available to generously offer workers training time and budget. This means the workers' motivation can vary drastically, depending upon the company. The reality is that no matter the size, few organisations provide enough incentives to encourage staff to continue their learning journey. So, for many workers, the answer to most of the questions posed here is not positive.

Worker's Motivation			
	Full-time	**Part-time**	**Freelance**
Incentive	Will learning provide better standing in the employee pool, promotion, improved satisfaction with work, better skills leading to easier execution of job, link to pay?	Will learning allow more flexibility or better pay? Will learning lead to better work?	
			Can training be used to enhance marketing?
Allocation of Time	Do the worker's objectives include assigned or optional training?	Is there time to acquire this competency? What is the cost/benefit (ROI)?	
Value of Training	Does the company market the positive outcome of its learning opportunities enough?	Are the benefits of the training tied clearly to increased marketability? Will training enable better or more stable part-time work?	
Perception of Training	Is training considered an essential component of every job and a critical responsibility for everyone in the company? Or is it seen as a reward for the luck few?	Is the specific training good value for money and time spent?	How can this training (certification, association standing) be leveraged to: • enable easier/ better marketing/ sales of skills? • obtain better work? • increase rates?

Table #03: Workers' Motivation

Until recently, most training systems required people to attend lengthy 12- to 24-month programmes held during evening or on weekends. The advent of online learning, lot-of-one training platforms and MOOC's, that allow participants to view lectures in real-time and interact with other students from around the world, have challenged this classic approach. Today, the world is full of learning, and life-long learning, opportunities and options.

But let's face it, only a minority of people are capable of embarking upon and completing an individualised transformational training programme using online tools. We all know the issues. First, this type of learning requires a very high level of motivation, since it is done on personal time. Second, dedicating personal time to keeping your job, or training up for a 'possible' future position does not really match the new generation's perspective of work-life balance. In addition, no matter which path is chosen, it is slow. Very slow.

Let's compared this to the decision-making process that organisations use to implement new technology, digital factory interfaces, or productionline automation. A typical lapse between decision and rollout is only about 9 to 18 months. Shocking, when compared to the traditional training time lapse of 12 to 24 months; by the time the skills are acquired, it is a real possibility that the job has already been filled, or the worker has already lost their position. For a burning platform to be effective, the worker must have enough time to upskill, so they have somewhere to land when they jump out of the embers. The length of time most traditional training and/or reskilling takes precludes any meaningful transition.

Main Messages

Change is not comfortable for most people. Should your job be at risk in 'company A', you might envisage that you could always just move to company B. Jumping companies to maintain employment with obsolete skills could become the norm in most workplaces. The issue these days is the probability that the job with 'company B' could also disappear. The OECD Future of Work report indicates that countries and business are putting more focus on professions with systematically lower risk of automation[2]. Germany, for example, where close to 40% of all employees have undergone at least one occupational re-qualification, is moving its workers away from higher-risk jobs.

Freelance and independent workers are on the rise, investing more in their own competencies, they are no longer available for traditional full-time employment. Even with full employment, we do not see the percentage of part-time workers reducing sharply; so part-time work is also eating away at millions of potential hours that normally could be allocated to full-time worker. This convergence of trends is making it even more difficult to attract resources, especially if the traditional employee pool might be halved. It is becoming a seller's market for knowledge workers. Money, time, training, can be leveraged to combat this imbalance. Re-qualification and reskilling are important tools to transition towards jobs that have a lower likelihood of being automated, but there is still quite an important element required; the willingness and motivation of workers to embark on this type of learning journey.

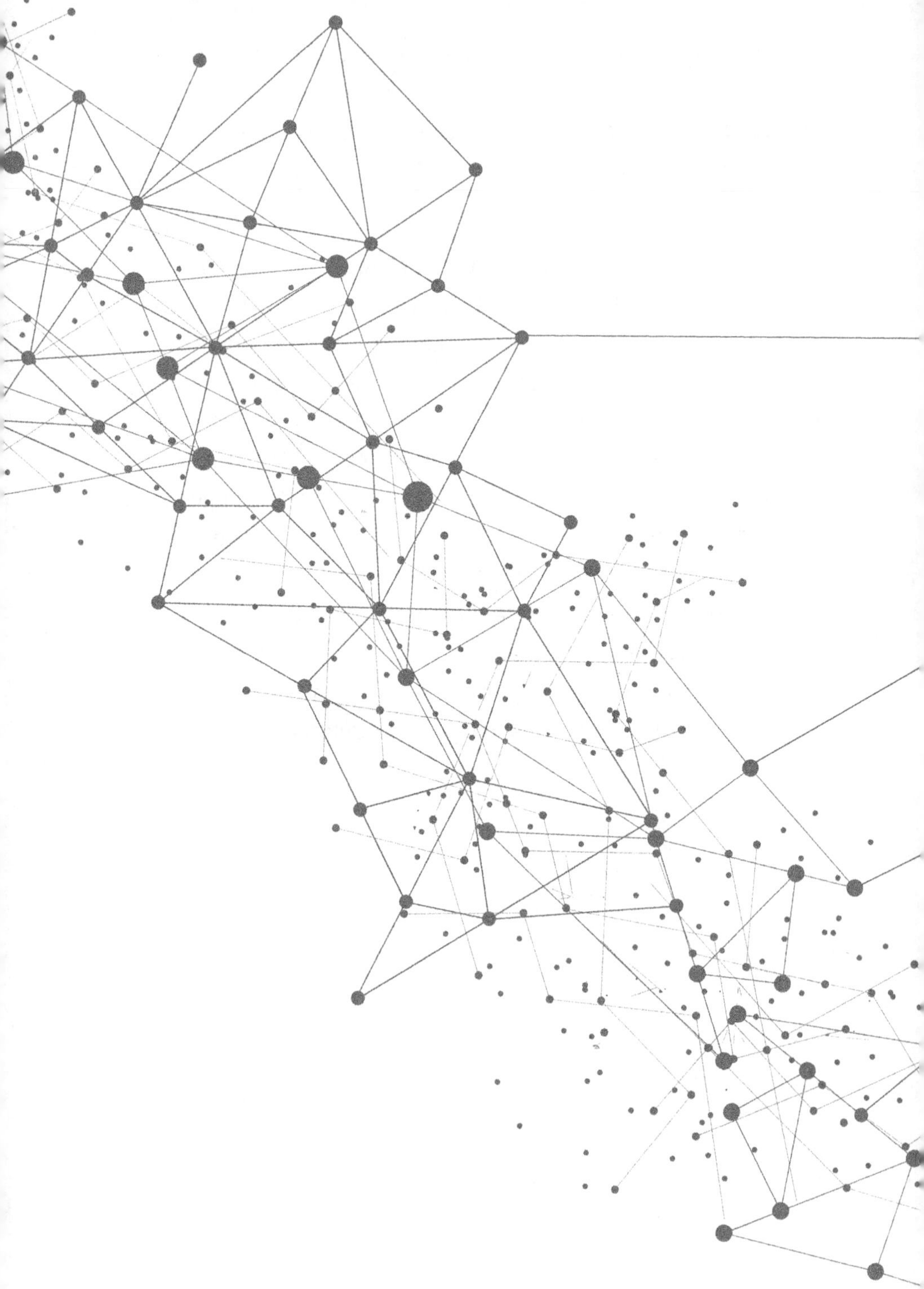

Section II:
6 Steps, The Upskilling Solution

KEY CONCEPTS

Individuals
- Make worker central to upskilling initiative
- New job perspective is a must
- Qualitative & quantitative measures, concrete actions & agreements will support worker engagement

Government
- Holistic approach: all sectors, all companies, all people
- Supporting regulations and incentives
- Positive communication: rationale, drivers & expected optimistic future
- High return on investment for all

Organisations
- Collaboration between worker, organisation & government is critical to success
- the CEO's main role is strategic, stakeholder consultation is critical
- New internal mobility framework and organisation

Figure 06: Upskill! A 6 Step Solution

Chapter 5: Successful Upskilling: 6 Steps

Upskilling is powerful but must be executed with the correct strategy. The upskilling solution can be tailored to resolve issues for countries, regions, corporations, industries and individuals, but it must be supported by a regulatory framework and a vibrant job market. Our hope is that this simple roadmap will help leaders to strategize and execute successful upskilling plans. This chapter presents an overview of these steps, their respective objectives, associated activities and expected outcomes.

Keys to Success

Using our learning from our extended review of different international initiatives afforded us the opportunity to understand the complexity and risks of upskilling. This 6-Step method matured over time and was strengthen by the lens of experience formed as we implemented successful upskilling initiatives. Successful upskilling is achieved by completing 6 steps in a specific order.

Step 1: Analyse & Define Upskilling Initiative

Step 2: Design Workforce Skills Plan

Step 3: Perform Individual Employee Assessment & Provide Advice

Step 4: Engage Workers & Match Jobs (the new science)

Step 5: Select & Provide Training

Step 6: Monitor, Evaluate & Improve Policy

Overarching activities throughout the process include strategy assessment and evaluation, communication plan monitoring, and policy improvements. This virtuous continuous improvement circle provides the bedrock for the methodology.

Upskilling Sponsorship

Upskilling initiatives are kicked off and led by visionary leaders who have reflected deeply upon the long-term business and social elements that sustain growth in their region, country or industry. Upskilling strategies can originate with industry, association or political leaders. Whatever the origins of these leaders' ideas, they have considered and are deeply committed to generating sustainable growth through the development of intellectual capital and the optimisation and enhancement of workforce skills.

An example of leadership in this area is President Macron's initiative to dedicate an enormous national budget to new vocational training. This programme was supported by sweeping changes to the regulatory framework that accelerates and expands upskilling. The Luxembourg government's upskilling initiative is another prime illustration of a leader's potential impact. The Minister of Labour, Nicolas Schmit, launched a multi-stakeholder pilot project that was supported by trade unions and trade associations. This pilot focused on upskilling 'at-risk' employees, vulnerable to the introduction of new technology.

Being able to come to consensus when/if major challenges arise is critical to the successful implementation of any upskilling initiative. Visionary leaders easily gather different stakeholders around the table to mobilise important conversations. Gaining agreement through discussion, alignment regarding common ground and collaborative action is critical to the successful execution of the 6 steps.

Step 1: Analyse & Define Upskilling Initiative

Objective: Define the upskilling strategy within a country, region, industry or a corporation.

Outcome: Precise scope, budget, implementation and stakeholder engagement plan.

Planning is synonymous with success. Preparatory steps are an essential element in the success of any upskilling initiative. The objective of this first step is to define the upskilling strategy and with it, the relevant execution plans and resources. The expected outcomes are precise; scope, budget, implementation and stakeholder engagement plan.

For this step, we would strongly recommend applying design thinking methodology, which allows stakeholders to conceptualise, co-create and prototype new products, services, strategies, and business models. This methodology builds on deep insights and feedback from employee, corporate and governmental user groups. Considering stakeholders, systems, the scale of regulatory framework, human factors, initiative inputs, required outcomes, and their relation to upskilling objectives, is a powerful tool for engaging the community in prototyping and testing. This feasibility step is composed of six modules.

Module 1.1: Understand Context & Drivers

Upskilling cannot be discussed without deep consideration of context. It is very important for all stakeholders to understand influencing factors that will impact the upskilling approach. An organisation is influenced by factors in their region and industry; manufacturing activities, market conditions, sales methodology, workforce availability, governmental and other support mechanisms. A workforce upskilling strategy in northern Sweden, therefore, will be as different from a strategy in southern Sweden, as the industry value chain and job markets are in the two regions. Even if we are undertaking upskilling initiatives in the same industry, automotive for instance, the upskilling strategy in Baden Württemberg is as different from upskilling in Slovakia, as their production activities and value chains. Upskilling requirements vary dramatically across locations, industries and even between different organisations.

This module provides context for leaders to assess how supportive the environment and framework are, and the level of key stakeholder engagement: employees, workers, corporate leaders, trade unions and trade associations. Understanding the context consists of analysing local job market perspectives...

- What are the CEO's expectations and strategic objectives (for example, downsizing or upscaling operations) and intentions and/or thoughts on upskilling and internal mobility?

- Is the market well-oriented to job creation, or is it more pessimistic with corporate social plans?

- Which industry is looking for talent and which has overcapacity?

- What is the appetite of trade unions and business associations for upskilling?

- How supportive to upskilling are existing regulatory and financial mechanisms?

An independent consultation of CEOs by core industry in the region, can provide a plethora of objective information for analysing the environment. The outcomes of these consultations are compiled, shared and discussed in a multi-stakeholder forum to build a common vision. Two key dimensions are critical; stakeholder engagement and enabling frameworks. Analysis of these dimensions provide direction (see illustration below).

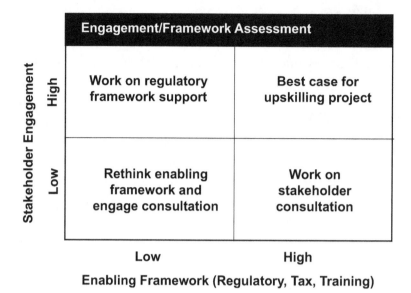

Figure #07: Engagement/Framework Assessment

1. **Best Case**: If stakeholder engagement is high and enabling framework conditions (regulatory framework, financial incentives, vocational training quality etc.) are well-developed, it provides the support essential to success, and therefore, no corrective actions are required. The upskilling initiative can leverage the existing 'goodwill' perspective and/or approaches that will already pervade the stakeholder groups, therefore facilitating the initiative's immediate launch.

2. **Stakeholder Consultation**: When the enabling framework (regulatory, financial, etc.) is strong, it provides a supportive platform for the project. Yet if stakeholder engagement is weak, or the consultation process was not sufficiently participative or engaging, an additional stage – consultation and discussion with stakeholders – is necessary to understand and eradicate any barriers to upskilling. Deeper stakeholder engagement may surface political, social and economic reasons that may be blocking support. If stakeholder engagement

is effective, it provides a roadmap for addressing existing issues and rallies the support of individuals and groups for the project. It is very difficult to oppose an upskilling initiative if you know everyone's concerns and interests are being considered.

3. **Work on Enabling Frameworks**: Strong stakeholder engagement, but a weak enabling framework (regulatory, financial, etc.) is quite a common situation. When the regulatory framework does not provide strong support, or even blocks the upskilling initiative, it limits the breadth or depth of interventions. Adaptation is required.

   A good example of this is the Ministry of Labour in Luxembourg. The Ministry extended the scope of financing to training of employed individuals (versus training only for the unemployed population) to support the upskilling initiative. This degree of flexibility and the ability to modify measures and regulations is critical to upskilling success.

4. **Rethink**: The worst-case scenario is when stakeholder engagement is low and the enabling framework (regulatory, finance, etc.) do not support an upskilling initiative. In this case, the problem is far larger than just upskilling and requires a full review of economic and labour policies coupled with grassroots action to catalyse stakeholder engagement.

No matter how positive the landscape seems, it is critical to be vigilant that no group is 'left behind'. Constant dialogue and creative thinking keep the initiative on track, and leaders in touch with their constituency. Conversely, no matter how negative the situation may appear during the initial assessment, there are remedies and actions that can be used to build enabling regulations and engage stakeholder groups. If your community is ready to build for the future. It can happen!

Module 1.2: Define Scope, Objectives, Budget

During module 1, an independent consultant collects, assesses, and records the leader's intentions in terms of technology investment and how that will translate into addressing short-term and future skills requirements. This provides valuable information used to define scope, objectives and budget requirements for the initiative.

The scope defines the breadth and depth of the initiative. There are a number of questions that must be answered to ensure the planning and design process is accurate, for example:

- Is the upskilling initiative open to all industries, companies and people?

- Is the initiative limited to some categories? For example, some programmes in France are limited to the unemployed or low-skilled labour

- Is the programme focused only on high-risk industries facing automation? (For example, financial services)

Objectives provide qualitative and quantitative measures for the upskilling initiative. The definition and calibration of objectives is essential for explaining eligibility criteria and budget considerations for a company's upskilling application. It is also required to develop and maintain open lines of communication with stakeholders. Objectives should always include quantitative measures such as a change in employment, for example, increasing employment by 70%. Considerations and questions include:

- What is the expected impact?

- How will government, corporations and employees define success?

- How will the business and economic landscape be different once the initiative is complete?

- How will we know when we have succeeded?

- What should be measured?

- How should we measure?

Quantitative objectives are relatively simple to define so it's easy to get carried away. Choose the minimum mandatory set of metrics needed to bring the most success, so you do not become bogged down in producing reports or measuring elements that provide little return. The key is using key messages to align everyone's vision of the most important elements. Productive communication is enhanced by focusing on key messages that explain the initiative's objectives easily and succinctly. Consider ...

1. Number of participating companies

2. Number of employees to be assessed and upskilled

3. Change in percentage of low-skilled workers

4. Percentage of internal mobility versus external mobility

For any investment in upskilling, the initiative objectives should indicate the direct return for the government, the company and for the individual. (see Chapter 6, Return on Investment) An estimate of the expected return on investment (ROI) for government and business is required to ensure ample financing. It can be disastrous to run out of funding before the first milestones allow you to show success.

Qualitative objectives drive engagement and motivate action. They help paint a picture of the positive future state. Like the quantitative objectives, they should include only the minimum mandatory set of requirements, measuring only the essential elements. Qualitative objectives might include:

- mitigating the social risk linked to job automation and/or accelerating upskilled workers' entry into jobs that have been chronically vacant

- demonstrating the importance and impact of skills portfolio development in preventing chronic unemployment

- engaging stakeholders in continuous improvement and innovation

- increasing community awareness regarding new job requirements

- improving the quality of training providers, using a 'learning by objective' approach that includes regular assessments and continuous improvement

- improving the government's ability to communicate its labour policy....

The definition of a preliminary budget indicates how serious the initiative is to a company and individuals. Upskilling Return on Investment and Financing Solutions are so important that they have their own chapters later in the book. Here we cover the political and promotional aspects of budget negotiations. If the budget forecasts that hundreds of euro (or dollars) will be spent on each individual, it is not an upskilling initiative. It is skills maintenance training. Given the amount of preliminary work required, the magnitude of training to be provided and the frequency of ongoing monitoring should be clarified and included in budget forecasts.

Large-scale initiatives can include several thousand employees. Decision-makers must understand that, on average, a minimum of €5,000 to €10,000 must be allocated to each worker. For smaller groups or the high-tech industry, budgets of around €25,000 to €30,000 are realistic.

Defining the State's Contribution

Government decision-makers will define the State's contribution. Whether it is 10%, 25% or 50%, the remainder constitutes the corporate investment. The State's contribution to the upskilling initiative is influenced by several factors: the availability of other support mechanisms for the programme, the wealth of the companies involved, the local and sometimes regional economic situation, the urgency of the problem, and potential negative impacts if the State does not act to support the initiative properly.

Aside from financial support, government involvement should also include technical assistance to monitor, supervise and assess the impact of the programme while:

- companies prepare their workforce competency development plans, to ensure the correct training programmes are selected

- employees identify new career opportunities inside or outside of the company, and select the correct path (training, etc.) to realise those opportunities

- industry provides a high-quality methodological framework that supports and even guarantees the success of the programme

Pilot Programme: A key recommendation is that governments and corporations interested in deploying upskilling initiatives, start with a pilot project which solves an easy upskilling challenge in a limited time. The pilot project could be open to any company that falls within its parameters (eg size and time limitations). The government should also draw up a set of policy recommendations informed by stakeholder feedback. The recommendations can include information about local/regional labour law frameworks, output from lessons learned exercises with companies and employees, and vocational training programme quality and performance assessments. For instance, the scope, objectives and methodology of Luxembourg's Skills Bridge pilot project, were defined through a design thinking and agile methodology involving HR executives and employees. It took many consultations with CEOs, trade unions and business associations.

During the Skills Bridge design thinking sessions (describe earlier), worker feedback was used to polish the pilot's process in Luxembourg. We found that workers were much more motivated to embark upon training when they were guaranteed a more sustainable position (lower risk of automation) upon completion of their learning journey. This gave us deeper insight into critical elements that can influence the success of any upskilling endeavour.

The rational for using this methodology was threefold: 1) engage as many people as possible to build support for the initiative, 2) design the best upskilling solution possible, and 3) identify *and* remove any hidden barriers that might block the project. Intense stakeholder consultation is highly recommended. It ensures all opinions, whether held by corporate leaders or employees, are surfaced. It fulfils the need for added reflection and productive 'soak-time' found in most innovative projects.

Module 1.3: Define & Adapt Supportive Mechanisms

Based on the outcome of the feasibility analysis, decision-maker(s) must consider adapting and improving conditions to support the upskilling initiative. A policy-maker has different levers to apply:

Threefold support: Providing technical assistance to companies, individual advice to employees, and financing for the training. The regulatory framework must allow for the provision of these three types of supports to ensure an efficient process focused on employability and on-boarding the worker in the new or transformed job.

Payment of the salary during the training: A mechanism to support the company during the upskilling initiative is a very important enabler.

While in training, the employee will not be able to do their job at all, or may be able to perform only half-time duties. The company incurs additional costs to replace the individual. Since the company continues to pay salaries during training, it is important to ensure that the regulatory framework provides a salary support mechanism. If it doesn't, steps should be taken to define new and more supportive regulations.

Securing the job transition: it is very likely that the employee will only be motivated and commit to upskilling if they have a guaranteed job and can see a smooth transition to it. In other words, the lower the risk to the employee, the higher the motivation. Before they engage in the training programme, the employee should receive a description of the proposed new job and a draft transition schedule. Once it is accepted by both parties, the job proposal is subject to the employee successfully completing the training, but the proposal in itself, is a strong motivator to keep the transition on track.

When the employee is moving to a different job inside the same company, or group, this is not as major a problem. For workers who are transitioning to a job with a different company, it is very important to put in place specific mechanisms to provide security and certainty to all stakeholders.

Support for new entrepreneurs: Some employees have a dream, or a passion outside of their job, and may be interested in moving toward a more entrepreneurial endeavour. Company reorganisations, and the evolution of tasks and functions, can be a great catalyst to trigger change. Enabling factors can include business plan reviews, initial funding mechanisms, benefits, social security, and pension continuity, in addition to business coaching and upskilling training for a specific period. This is a high-impact measure to support the somewhat daunting first step on the journey to becoming an entrepreneur.

A salary level guarantee: upskilling initiatives imply switching from one job to another. In some cases, especially when the worker will be required to switch companies, the salary for the new job might be lower than the job they are leaving. To foster and promote job mobility, compensation mechanisms must be in place to ensure the worker maintains the same or close to the existing salary level. This very important enabler significantly reduces mobility barriers.

Skills insurance plan: An individual skills insurance plan, which collects contributions from the employee as well as the employer, during the life-cycle of their career, represents a sustainable financing mechanism to upskill the workforce. It also helps to instil an understanding of the stakeholders' long-term responsibility regarding the employability of the workforce. The supportive mechanisms described in chapter #7, Financial Solutions, plays a critical role in the engagement of corporate decision-makers and employees.

Tax incentives: We also recommend defining tax incentives to support companies and employees. This could take the form of bonus pay-outs from the government, or tax breaks for employees who have successfully completed upskilling initiative. Organisations could also develop an enabling financial rewards framework used to enhance the regulatory framework supporting upskilling and participants' success.

Module 1.4: Define Governance

This module is strategic. It determines who will verify and select upskilling participants, validate the budget, and authorise support programmes. This defines the balance of power between stake-holders, influences their level of engagement, and impacts the speed and depth of the certification process required (including the level of transparency and confidentiality).

The Minister of Labour or Regional Head manages the gover-nance of national upskilling initiative. Given the importance of such programmes for workers and companies alike, and the funds at stake, special attention should be paid to this activity. The set-up and composition of the different committees which assess and val-idate the company's plans, must be organised with an eye to rapid decision-making, professional governance, and swift progress.

Transparency is a key success factor. It builds trust and demon-strates that any company can apply without discrimination. Pro-viding information via a website and ensuring that there is a clear application and selection process also adds credibility to the programme.

Confidentiality plays a major role in building trust. Company and worker applications and assessments are very sensitive. A breach in confidentiality or in data privacy could put the entire programme at risk. Consequently, we recommend that government officials only be involved in decision-making, and not the process itself. As well as limiting exposure of sensitive information streamlining processes to include only essential actors, ensures that processes are shorter, simpler and easier to organise and execute.

Module 1.5: Define Execution Strategy & Stakeholders

For an initiative to be successful, a full execution strategy must be defined. The operationalisation of the plan, including detailed milestones, is critical to maintaining momentum. High-quality, responsive and professional services can also form a solid base for success. The execution of an upskilling initiative can be assigned to a public agency, but the speed and quality of project activities must reach international corporate standards. To accomplish this, the public agency selects private consultants, trained in the methodology, to assist in this phase. This is particularly necessary during the set-up and implementation of any new software used for the workforce planning and assessment. Based on our experience, implementing software in a government IT infrastructure takes too long. Using Agile third-party providers to assist the public agency is a key success factor. The execution plan also considers multiplier roles and the tasks associated with trade associations, Chambers of Commerce, or trade unions. Having their support during the process of communicating with, and on-boarding of companies and workers reinforces the credibility of the initiative.

Module 1.6: Define Communication Plan

Communication is one of the most critical elements in any plan. It effectively allows workers to understand that they are a part of the story and that learning is an on-going process – for everyone in the company. Quite often companies fail to communicate major changes to their staff. They may even shy away from communicating about radical work or technology changes. Reasons for this run the gamut of protection against industrial competition, uncertainty regarding the project's deployment steps, or even the organisation not having a clear strategy about how it will handle the human resources side of the change. Here again, lack of transparency does not build confidence. In fact, it can create an atmosphere of fear and suspicion among employees. This is not helpful to the organisational change management team when the project is officially launched.

Even when the communication is executed flawlessly, we are still not entirely out of the woods. When it comes to the training itself, there are a variety of hurdles to overcome. Awareness is key. We are not talking about short training sessions, over in a few days or a week. Upskilling initiatives require the key influencers to understand the gravity of their project and ensure that workers' demands are considered. Learning is work, but it is a different type of work. Because of this, many participants may need support in crossing that two- to nine-months bridge and finalise their training.

Positive communication about the reskilling initiative and the project itself is a critical success factor. If the initiative is seen as positive and future-focused, it will be received more enthusiastically by the stakeholders. If it is seen as the last chance or last alternative before layoffs begin, resistance will build until it becomes, in many cases, insurmountable. It is no surprise that supporting the initiative with a positive, energetic communication campaign, is of utmost importance for workers' morale and to position the initiative in the most positive light possible.

From day one, the communication plan:

- enhances the urgency of action

- supports the development of the skills portfolio

- underlines the importance of rapidly filling job vacancies, and

- showcases role-model companies and employees who participate the upskilling initiative.

Communication should specifically address CEO and HR executives, unions and workers. Keep in mind that the objectives, actions, advantages of the initiative, and positive expected outcomes are different for these target groups. A detailed communication plan must include thoughtful consideration and effective description of the benefits to each stakeholder group. Without this detailed and very pragmatic list, many stakeholders will fail to understand the positive potential outcomes for themselves and others.

Step 2: Design Workforce Skills Plan

Objective: translate technology & digital investment plans into human capital development plans.

Outcome: forecast FTEs, future jobs (automation), & skills portfolio. Create annual diversity & workforce skills plan.

An important and critical finding during our research was that most organisations do not translate their technology and digital investment plans into a human capital development plan. No matter the sector, we found numerous examples of this omission. A large proportion of companies we met during our initial fact-finding were experiencing similar gaps in their workforce skills. External recruitment is a very difficult challenge when companies are competing for the same kind of rare profiles as every other organisation on the market – at the same time. Internal recruitment requires a much more sophisticated approach and becomes more important strategically than external recruitment. New methodologies and tools leverage artificial intelligence to focus on internal mobility and forecasting skills portfolio for workforce planning.

Module 2.1: Leveraging HR Technology

The acquisition of new technology significantly transforms the work in most organisation. This is especially true in terms of the number of staff engaged in new activities or jobs, and types of competencies required. A new generation of workforce planning tools are necessary to help HR executives forecast the degree of automation, future needs based upon the organisation's strategic direction, digital advancement, and anticipated task obsolescence.

These new tools exist. They are available today. Simply introducing an excel file containing all job listings into the new software, allows HR executives to obtain a snapshot of when and how their workforce may be transformed. The output from these tools helps the HR team to use third-party analysis, design different scenarios, define and challenge the transformation plan.

Business leaders are not always clear about the real impact of technology on their people. HR can expand their strategic contribution by forecasting personnel migration requirements and even proposing solutions based on the variables used in their analysis. These scenarios and plans can be reviewed against internal investment plans and the uptake rate of new technology.

Forecasting the number of FTEs using historical data such as staff turnover, pensions, new job creation and job reductions, is no longer sufficient. Creating an organisational forecast methodology that tracks the quality and quantity of competency portfolio changes is the new paradigm. This raises a basic, but very complex question: How to get these new competencies? And from where?

For the moment, this technology is only accessible to large companies mostly because of the cost, but there is room for workforce planning democratisation. SMEs, for example, could participate using customised governmental support mechanisms which might include vouchers and other upskilling collateral. This universal workforce planning platform is recommended for all companies, as wide-spread use would support more accurate national skills forecasting and plan development.

Using a 9- to 18-month project horizon for training and upskilling will, in reality, produce optimal returns on training investment and resource use. For many upskilling initiatives, the key ingredient is the worker's motivation to participate fully.

Example: SAP

SAP can never be accused of being late on the uptake of technology. In an interview for McKinsey Quarterly (November 2018), the SAP Chief HR Officer and Digital Business Services Head discussed the massive workforce skills upgrade that will ultimately encompass 20,000 employees, beginning with almost 5,000 in 2017. Taking a strategic planning and hiring approach, the executives talked about lessons learned and the engagement required for a global transformation that put learning and upskilling at its core. Tips for success include, start early, take incremental steps to achieve your goals, consider what support is needed for different target groups and ensure that all stakeholders are engages in the initiative[80]. One of the strongest messages we take from this example is the need for HR to not only support but lead the way in technology upskilling initiatives. Leading by example, they must be the first and most fervent supporters of upskilling[81].

The question on everyone's mind should be 'how many companies are undertaking annual workforce planning effort with a 1-year horizon?' According to our experience visiting hundreds of organisations, there is only a thin minority performing this exercise.

Module 2.3: Diversity and Workforce Skills Planning

Insufficient attention to diversity, and gender in particular, causes recurring issues such as lack of innovation, less creative thinking, and wastes an untapped talent pool; reckless human capital management in the best of economies. Upskilling can be particularly important to women as they will be disproportionately impacted by digitalisation and job automation.

Upskilling is one way to rapidly 'right-size' gender equality, balancing diversity within an organisation or institution. The 'full potential' scenario where women would have the same opportunity and hold identical roles as men in the labour market, indicates that $28 trillion would be added to the economy; an addition of 26% of GDP by 2025! In a business environment suffering from an accelerating 'war for talent' we cannot rule out the value of diversity.

Peruse your local shops or computer and you will find a plethora of books and articles on how to make this work. In terms of up-skilling initiatives, diversity promotion can be straight-forward. First and foremost, organisations must focus on the intent to increase diversity. Workforce skills planning must include diversity as a measurable goal. Regulations and policies must be (re)written *and* enforced, and sponsors found to endorsed and lead the diversity initiative. Personal coaching, management retraining and tar-geted communications can all be used to promote and formalise diversity-friendly behaviour. This area is one where government, community and association involvement is required. The upskilling initiative can connect with organisations such as Women in Digital Empowerment, Girls in Tech, Fit4Coding, etc. to establish and/or determine role models in the community who can encourage work-ers to step outside their comfort zone.

Example: IBM

IBM is a well-known success story, whose Diversity & Inclusion programme has lasted for decades. In 2018, the company won the Catalyst Award for Leadership, which recognised its efforts to build a workplace that values diversity and inclusion. But, as we all know, awards and written policies may just pay lip-service to a concept and may just be another marketing tool. Is there any hard evidence to warrant the award? Here again we look at the figures, in 1995 IBM launched an Executive Women's Diversity Task Force (one of the eight diversity-focused task forces started that year). Its objective was to improve women's opportunities for development and advancement through promoting cultural change, both at national and international levels[82]. By 1999, the number of women in executive positions had increased by 175% to reach 500.

IBM started numerous initiatives to attract and retain women in technology. It was recognised as the most LGBT-friendly employer in the world in 2016 (Workplace Pride Foundation). This population represents between 1% and 6% of the workforce (4.5% in the USA, 5.9% in Japan, and 2% in the UK.

Step 3: Perform Employee Assessment & Provide Advice

Objective: Assess employees, identify skills, achievements & motivation.

Outcome: Cross-fertilisation. Increased understanding of employee motivators & company's intent.

Today, best practice dictates that we perform a full individual assessment for each employee. This quantifies their skills, measures their career achievements and creates understanding regarding their personal and professional aspirations. The exercise provides clues to a variety of factors that might influence a worker's skills portfolio, and their motivation towards the company and future jobs. A vertical skills analysis links to current job activities, soft and digital skills, while feedback from the worker gives insight into professional and personal career aspirations, which are potentially very different from their current job. In parallel, new jobs or tasks are identified and the required skills quantified.

In a truly collaborative approach, the committed employee and employer work together to create the employee's individual skills development plan. This plan defines the steps and the training required to address the gap between the current employee skills portfolio and the new job requirements. For this to be effective, employee engagement must be optimised.

This assessment process allows companies to identify people who are more motivated to transfer jobs and/or participate in an upskilling. For example, a bank employee could use this exercise to flag their intention to completely switch careers. Following an external training programme would lead to employment outside of the financial industry.

Job matching is complex and brings with it a plethora of issues. Very few companies capture all this employee information on a regular basis, and therefore, it is much more difficult to find the best match for a new job-class or tasks. Comprehensive personnel assessments are highly strategic information gathering and classification. Taking the time to do a detailed analysis allows companies to better organise internal mobility and to match new jobs to people who previously, would never have been considered. This process is not about creating a way to circumvent layoff mechanisms, or to push people to do things they are not willing or capable of doing. It must be part of the normal company life-cycle and the employer's responsibility to look further into the future to address activities that could negatively impact the company's bottom-line and their workers' livelihoods.

It is important to remember that, depending on national legislation, this can be quite a sensitive topic that often triggers union attention. Here again, setting a positive atmosphere regarding the upskilling initiative is key, so the way the company engages in dialogue with the employees' representatives must be transparent.

Workers who need to upskill and who, in fact, feel that they are in charge of their own re-skilling are an important component of upskilling initiatives. The French government designed an intervention that ensures this group is upskilling in collaborate with their organisation, by making the individual central to the system. A new law passed on 1 August 2018, created an Individual Training Account, where workers can accumulate 'training funds'. Employers provide €5,000 or €8,000 (for non-qualified and qualified workers respectively) over a ten-year period and the worker has access to these funds for training. Workers only need approval from their employer if they take training during work hours.

This collaboration of workers being responsible for guiding their own development and using their personal time, and employers providing the training fund and approval when necessary, empowers both sides. It reduces barriers to training and provides enough incentive for most workers to further their skills! Included in this service are training proposals, approved providers for short maintenance training lasting from a few hours to a few days, and technical training providers (eg software, language refresher courses, regulatory changes or additions that are mandatory to learn, etc. that typically last longer).

Providers offer a variety of training modes; from classroom, to online or blended solutions. This allows workers to select the mode that best fits their schedule and situation. Do we really believe that letting everyone pick up training for a few hours without any real professional goals agreed with corporations will create the right skills? In the absence of clear shared skills strategy by the government and organisations, workers tend to gravitate toward training that addresses their own personal interest but might be totally ineffective from a career perspective.

What about individuals who need more than a few days of training? Is there an effective way to handle major upskilling efforts? For exaple, the accountant who wishes to become a data protection analyst, or the software engineer wishing to transition to a cyber-security analyst position?

Confidence and fear are main drivers that influence one's ability to transition effectively. It is logical to look at upskilling training for new and/or very different jobs with some anxiety. It is normal to have doubts. And there can be many for a worker;

- Will they be able to achieve the required level to make it worth-while?

- Has it been too long since they were last in training or learned new skills?

- How will the length of time it takes to acquire the skill be re-flected in their CV?

- How will the ensuing period of 'unemployment' on their resume be perceived?

- What if they fail? Will they get a second chance?

- Are the rules clear enough for them to make an informed and correct decision?

- What is the certainty of really having a job when the training is completed?

These are all legitimate concerns, but time and time again, we see that workers are much more motivated to embark on training when they are guaranteed a more sustainable position with lower risk of automation upon completion of their learning journey. We have heard the questions listed above from many workers. Organisa-tions and the upskilling initiative team must consider them while designing the project and communication plans. Many workers might prefer to go to a familiar job in 'company B' rather than engage in three to four months of training for a more sustainable job requiring more skills. The execution of a well-thought-through assessment programme – that includes personal coaching and advice, can go a long way to assuage the worker's fears and allow them to move to an improved, more sustainable position. This simple assessment step enables workers to rapidly transfer to new jobs by ensuring a better match between their interests and knowledge of domains required for new job.

Step 4: Engage Workers & Match Jobs (the new science)

Objective: Match employees (existing skills, motivation, profile alignment) to future jobs.

Outcome: Increased employee mobility. Upskilling contract between worker & organisation with future job.

Step #4 matches workers who have the highest motivation, profile alignment and existing skills, to potential jobs.

Module 4.1: Leveraging Technology

New job matching tools that use artificial intelligence, now make real-time recommendations about workers who are the best fit for a job. This disruptive software innovation (eg riminder, dynajob, seedlink, leap, etc.) allows HR personnel, or even employees themselves, to upload a full profile onto a platform that uses deep machine-learning techniques to select suitable vacancies and seamlessly match them to the candidate. Automatic reports from these systems allow HR executives to stay apprised of developments in job or position requirements and to be assured that the best candidates are being found and considered. Just like dating, it's rare to find the perfect match so the software quantifies the skills gap between the candidate and job requirements. This new matching process between skills, motivation and job requirements allows a 'best fit' approach to job searches.

Given the nature of rapidly emerging technology, much of the performance and validation testing that will be used to assess the relevance and reliability of these new AI matching tools must still be conducted by HR and other AI specialists. The main benefit is that these tools help avoid bias when selecting people for a job. The beauty of the system is that it discovers people who might never consider applying for the job and, on the company side, tap into a new pool of talents with the right skills portfolio and potential.

This allows the company to assess the worker's or recruitment candidate's potential in a different, broader manner. It assesses current skill sets and considers the potential of every recruit and worker. Further, the true potential of this approach is that everyone involved with personnel management and/or planning becomes more strategic. They come to realise that there is no way to predict with 100% accuracy how jobs will evolve and what skills will be required even 3 years into the future. A better assessment of current employees' and recruits' potential is a good investment in future performance. Understanding your team's abilities and their interest in learning, gives a clear indication of their mobility potential.

Module 4.2: Employee Engagement

Employee engagement connects the employee solidly with their new career path. First, the sign-off for the individual skills development plan defines the training plan and confirms agreements. A secured transition to the new job (signing a new work contract or mobility letter of agreement between the worker and potential/ future employer before the start of training) builds the employee's full engagement. It also significantly increases the employee's commitment to the training process. Individual, independent personal career advice is also great reassurance for the employee.

As an example: a compliance officer in a bank, is being replaced by a set of automated processes. Through the bank upskilling initiative, John identifies different job opportunities inside the bank such as risk management officer or data officer. An external compliance consulting manager position with in a large international professional services firm is also a match. Given the conclusions drawn from his personal skills assessment, John is inspired by the external opportunity but is apprehensive about changing companies and facing a job shift, after 20 years with the bank. He is also a bit concerned with the three month intense training. The consulting firm offers him a contract for the new job, subject to the success of his training.

John, after consultation with his personal advisor, accepts the job offer and starts the training. His advisor touches base with him during the training to confirm that he is feeling positive about his development and to monitor his upskilling progress. After the training, John meets the external HR executive (of the professional services firm) to review his plan and his on-boarding schedule.

Following a three month trial period, John is permanently hired. His new firm, pays him a special welcome package and bonus, after he successfully completes on-boarding and the trial period. The bonus is equivalent to 50% of the recruitment costs saved by the firm using candidates from the national upskilling initiative.

Step 5: Select & provide training

Objective: Ensure streamlined, effective training programme to upskill workers

Outcome: High level of employability & worker motivation. Effective collaboration between worker, corporation, association/unions & government

A key success factor in all upskilling initiatives is ensuring that the training provided to workers is of the highest quality and is an effective and efficient way to help them take on a new function. Ensuring a high level of employability generates massive savings for the State and for companies. High employability also makes a huge difference in the employee's outlook and motivation. Upskilling initiatives offer us the opportunity to reverse vocational training markets from a supply-based, to a market-driven model that is focused on the real needs of companies and people.

Moule 5.1: Training Selection

But how can we ensure that training providers are responsive to the future needs of jobs and the upskilling initiative? Transparency, stimulation of competition and communication constitute the core elements of the training provider's market approach. Communicating the needs of the upskilling initiative to training providers, including the importance of skills-acquisition-focused objectives is key. Launching requests for proposals to all training providers will cause them to progressively adapt and innovation their traditional offering.

Example: Sheffield

In Sheffield (UK), the Skills Bank aims to support and encourage Sheffield City Region employers to develop their business through savvy investments in their staff's skills training. Its mission is to forecast the digital skills training needs of SMEs and to consolidate training offers. Here, the training model is fully adapted to local needs. Instead of having to purchase training for their staff from a standard training catalogue, companies in Sheffield district, can make a precise request to the Skills Bank, which launches several results- and performance-driven calls for tenders. An operator, interfacing with the market, ensures that training solutions best match the company's requests. In addition, the Sheffield Skills Bank can fund up to 70% of the training, provided the participant matches the eligibility criteria.

Starting with £4.82 million of core funding from the local government and another £22 million from the Business Investment Fund, part of a larger National growth hub initiative funded by the central government (with access to £90 million in funding) the overall goal is to create 70,000 new jobs and 6,000 new businesses by 2025[83].

The key elements of this regional upskilling initiatives are a:

- dedicated helpline for employers to identify the best training for their staff

- funding model with contribution from local, national and EU government funding, as well private (business) investment

- new generation skills assessment tool, and

- selection of training providers that work to very specific skills objectives and guarantees quality and value for money

Since March 2016, more than 2,000 people had joined this scheme, and another 10,000 were in the pipeline[84] (Sheffield City Region Skills Bank). It has provided 77 masterclasses (marketing & sales, technology, tendering, etc.) and supported 366 business[85]. The new-generation programmes scored higher on quality and satisfaction than previous ones. The Skills Bank enables businesses to grow through access to new skills. This indicates that it is possible to find the right set-up using local and online resources to upskill people within two to nine months.

Module 5.2: Medium-term Training Provision

Upskilling initiatives also offer the opportunity to find and support corporate training programmes including those specialised in new technology. The key criteria for selecting professional training programmes are market recognition, their track record, and the trust built with corporations through placing well-trained staff in new jobs. In terms of curricula, the upskilling initiative contains three major pillars:

Vertical Curriculum: The vertical curriculum directly relates to the new job and is provided by the hiring company or an external training provider. Through our consultation with industry, we found that several European manufacturers have recently reshaped their full curriculum library to meet their new technology and skills requirements.

Learning Factories: New training programmes can be associated with production line investments. Corporate academies use the Learning Factory concept to train workers on new-generation production lines. Well worth the cost when we consider the millions invested in new technology.

Government Support: The magnitude of required investment for industry training activities clearly limits the capacity of third-party providers, and private or trade association, to offer the same quality infrastructure. Some companies, given the correct incentive, are happy to offer their training programme to the market. The government can support industrial manufacturers, encouraging them to open their new training facilities to stakeholders in the local value chains.

If a company plans to install new robotic process automation (RPA), customer relationship management (CRM), automated warehouse, robot, or even 3D printers, decisions must be made and almost 'frozen' in time, about 9 to 18 months before any new technology is set up. The purchase order is signed and the selection process for the provider is underway long before anything happens on site.

Training to the medium-term (9 to 18 months) then becomes a key strategic factor if the company wishes to prepare workers. If the company starts too soon, for example two to three years before, it is too far in advance because decision-making will still be uncertain and, therefore, the team will lack the burning platform that is used to rally workers. The 9- to 18-month horizon gives the project team (or HR) adequate time to organise efficient and cost-effective training, and workers sufficient time to commit to and begin their learning journey. Waiting until a couple of months before the new tech is set up, is too late for all this to happen effectively.

Module 5.3: Ongoing Digital Upskilling

The reality is that all employees, no matter what their job is today, must upskill regularly on digital technologies and applications. Upskilling initiatives allow at least a minimum mandatory allocation of two days of technical training per participating employee per year. The inclusion of software-provider training programmes is a key element to success.

Given the complexity and multitude of areas and programmes, we suggest using accepted international frameworks such as the European Computer Driver's licence which offers modules with diagnostic tests, adaptive learning tools, eLearning and links to several well-recognised software training providers. Their quality-focus on new technologies, and skills building, represents a common international language that enables people globally to learn their software and use their programmes.

Let's look at a couple of examples; one in technology and another that uses a skills bank to accelerate local upskilling efforts. This first example is about teaching participants to code computer applications and programmes. Is it possible for someone who knows nothing about coding to become good enough in three months to get hired? Believe it or not, it seems to be very possible to learn to code in 9 to 15 weeks with excellent outcome in terms of employment. There are multiple examples of coding schools where no technical knowledge is required to gain a spot. Participants are selected based on their motivation *and* cognitive skills. The coding courses have proven to be very successful; due, at least in part, to the full-time training approach. Daily tests, immediate remediation for issues and individual real-time follow up, real cases and projects, set these programmes apart. At the end of the two- to three-month curriculum, most students find a job.

This format is becoming a world phenomenon. It is working so well and becoming so popular, that it has exploded with franchising, rankings, and more and more organisations joining the business sector, etc.[86] It's not just a pattern emerging in the USA. In France people are also talking about the 'boom of web schools'[87]. In 2014, Progate launched its online coding school in Japan. It's programme, comprised of AI, robotics and customer interface, attracted more than 200,000 users in the first three years of operation[88]. One might posit that this success is limited to only IT-related fields. But we are currently investigating and testing our upskilling cycle with companies (in Luxembourg) that are drastically modifying or changing their production methods.

From projects to develop 'the factory of future', to new technology on production lines, the same patterns play out. We see this in other industrial sites visited within 20 EU countries. Lack of personnel forces upskilling. Since it's quite difficult to find qualified workers with very specific knowledge, companies are choosing to invest in tailored training programmes to bring either existing, familiar or newly recruited workers up to the required competency level. It takes from a few weeks to nine months in the situations we have witnessed. The programmes are usually full-time and fully supported by the company. The worker is offered a tailored training programme where they can learn to operate machines, for example, in the Industry 4.0 format. This training programme happens before the technology is introduced and in a reasonable timeframe, that provides both the employer and employee visibility and confidence that expectations are achievable.

Module 5.4: Soft Skills Acquisition

Soft skills are major category and 'low hanging fruit' for an upskilling initiative. Due to heavy employee workloads, many companies might be reluctant to provide two or three days of soft skills training to everyone in the organisation. Even some employees might hesitate to take this amount of time off for soft skills training. This is one of the major benefits of a national upskilling initiative. The OECD study on skills and global value chain concludes that 'to integrate and grow in global markets, all industries need workers who have not only strong cognitive skills (including literacy, numeracy and problem solving), but management and communication skills, as well as a readiness to learn'. A tailored soft skills programme focused on key mandatory topics for all employees helps engage the whole population in a virtual circle of improving communication, and teamwork. It also forms a solid foundation for life-long learning.

Step 6: Monitor, Evaluate & Improve Policy

Objective: Ensure transversal continuous improvement & communicate successes.

Outcome: Streamlined programme administration, market alignment, 'good news' stories, clear understanding of potential jobs scenarios, clear return on investment.

Let's pause here a minute. When workers are sent to training, what type of follow-up or support do they receive from their direct supervisors? We have all witnessed that in normal conditions, supervisors, often forgetting about the training, discover the worker's absence the same day (or just before) and await their return to the 'real' job with impatience. We rarely witness a phone call or meeting aimed at conducting a post-training debrief, to better understanding what the worker has learned or their plan for implementing the new skills.

Although this is not yet a normal part of the average supervisor's toolkit, it's time for a rethink. An upskilling initiative requires workers to embark upon what can be a very stressful endeavour. The supervisor's support and sponsorship are directly transmitted through the communication style and messaging they use. So is their approval for the training. But is this sufficient? Other support can include HR or even an external advisor or coaches well-versed in the type of personal challenges and/or issues that arise for participants during an upskilling initiative.

Module 6.1: HR's Role

HR's position as a business partner is now quite widespread. One of their responsibilities is to know and understand workers in their business division and to follow special cases. Worker who are starting a long training programme are clearly worth this attention. Tackling the administrative burden; ensuring that registrations are completed correctly and delivered in a timely manner, anticipating potential trips, and payroll issues is a small part of the service they can offer. HR can lead discussions aimed at ensuring that the company's investment is well-placed and that the worker has the right skills and attitude to take on the training, before decisions are taken. HR can also ensure that management is aligned, and that social representatives are informed and supportive.

Another important aspect of HR's role is assigning personnel to support workers emotionally as they follow their training path. This requires special attention, but also some specialised HR systems, if it is to be done at scale. Indeed, following dozens or hundreds of workers, in a variety of personal situations and locations during the same period, is almost impossible without proper HR tools. HR must know who attends which programme and what specific training each worker is receiving, at any given time. It is critical to confirm that workers are really attending the training, and not 'dropping the pen' due to stress or difficulty in following the curriculum. Monitoring all these aspects of the training is critical to supporting the worker.

Module 6. 2: Support Upskilling Participants

Workers may not always be willing or capable of sharing deeply personal feelings and issues with their employer, or HR, which can be seen as a representative of the company. It is difficult for most people to admit they have doubts about their choices or misgivings about moving forward.

During our design thinking sessions with workers, we found that the presence and support of an external advisor was a clear asset during a lengthy training programme. Another winning tactic expressed in the sessions, was to group workers together who are going through similar experiences during the training. Social support via virtual platforms, enables workers to ask questions, to identify with, and provide support to, others going through the same pain or doubts. Guided by a personal advisor, this method of interaction can also enable small groups to reflect on specific, but important, factors associated with their journey, such as how to:

-   rest and revitalise themselves during the long-term programme

-   catch-up with classwork in case of illness

-   to show solidarity for someone who is absent due to family or health issues

Module 6.3: Monitoring Platforms

This transversal phase of monitoring and communication from initiation to communicating successful job placement is critical. It is supported by a digital platform, which provides real-time information to government programme administrators, HR executives of participating companies, and employees. It provides key performance indicators for the five steps described above. For example;

- individual skills assessment module indicates the level of competencies and motivation of the workforce

- workforce planning tools monitor corporation forecasts regarding number of employees and their competency development

- job matching tools provide an overview of the different job opportunities for all participating employees

- consolidation of the individual skills development plans provides a clear overview of the required skills to fill new/vacant jobs in any given marketplace

- training platform documents the training journey of all participants, tracks skills acquisition daily progress and captures training costs. This provides participating governments with a full set of statistics and evidence such as trainings attended and passed

The communication platform used by all stakeholders consolidates best practices from participating corporations. It groups participants profiles by benefits realised through their learnings journey, via good news and success stories. Tips from individual advisers are posted, job opportunities presented, and key features associated with the selected curriculum of approved training providers made available.

Module 6.4: Upskilling & GDPR

The advent of GDPR and the great attention it is given, puts even more pressure on the employer. The upskilling initiative carries with it very personal and sensitive data related to skills, self-motivation, willingness to learn (or even to continue to work with the current employer). Here again, the employer must be willing to get this process right. They must guarantee workers that their personal data is safe and clearly explain who has access to what information and for what period of time. Technology is a great help here as encryption and privacy settings can automatically safeguard information.

Module 6.4: Institutionalising Upskilling

Once the upskilling initiative enters the critical phase of on-boarding upskilled employees, the communication strategy actively supports all success stories via a trans-media platform. Media stories follow individual employees in their upskilling journey. The government, participating companies and employees see successes, enhancements and employees are showcased as role models, as they take on new internal and external positions. This communication strategy plays a key role in transforming people's mindset.

Module 6.5: Changing the System

Governments learn quite a bit about the limits of their current labour and vocational training frameworks through dialogue with corporations and from employee behaviour. The Minister of Labour is bound to receive external feedback aimed at improving budget efficiencies. This is a major opportunity for the government to reinforce its country's competitiveness and capacity for growth.

The Minister of Education also receives a clearer view of the future skills gaps that must be closed. This is incredibly important if the higher education system is to provide the right skills for the country and its economy. Associating higher education with the upskilling initiative is an opportunity to reinforce the concept of partnerships with the industry. The Minister of Education can introduce the development of new competency centres at universities or ask for new generation learning tools in schools. (see Chapter 11, Educational Priorities for more details)

Main Messages

The upskilling cycle illustrated here shows a national framework, corporate growth, and employability elements for workers. Both frames are powered by new skills and include elements aimed at boosting economic growth and social inclusion. The steps provide a practical, fool-proof methodology for ensuring that the working population in every country is able and progress with changing times, and technology.

This is a critical element. Adaptability, leading to employability, is a central challenge for workers. In the scenarios we used here, the employer intervenes before the workers' 'obsolescence'. The worker invests in their skills to maintain the required level to be of service to the company.

The scenarios are all positive. Yet sometimes, by acting late, or worse, communicating at the last minute, the company can create distrust or cause stakeholders, such as unions, to send ambiguous or even negative messages to their workers. The wrong initial set-up or oversight, off-target communication, or discussions, will inevitably require added effort to engage workers positively. It will frustrate efforts and slow adoption of the mindset that supports upskilling efforts. To ensure efforts have a positive outcome, the upskilling initiative should include:

For the employee:

- a national initiative led by the government and hierarchical

- positive communication with, and from, supervisors, ensuring that workers feel supported during the project. They are the workers' first line of support

- a positive employee mind-set that keeps an open mind and asks for help when needed

- positive interaction with and behaviour of management and other stakeholders

- strong support for the workers' upskilling decision, through execution and right up to completion

- external support during the worker's critical decision-making (eg embarking on and during training) guided by standardised rules for all personnel advisors, and organised communication with the company

For the company:

- positive and effective communication regarding the project ensures a journey that will motivate and energise participants

- transparency about the project and its consequences. There is no place in upskilling initiatives for words like 'layoff' or 'last chance'. These words instil fear, provoke employee push-back and diminish the union's ability to offer support

HR also plays a key role by:

- setting clear rules on participation

- securing future jobs

- monitoring the workers' participation

- intervening through coordination with all stakeholders

Finally, the upskilling initiative should be supported by the tools that organise, monitor, register and ensure data privacy as needed. We cannot stress enough how important initial and ongoing communication is to the successful completion of the project. It will influence the workers' willingness at the beginning of the project, and their resilience during its execution.

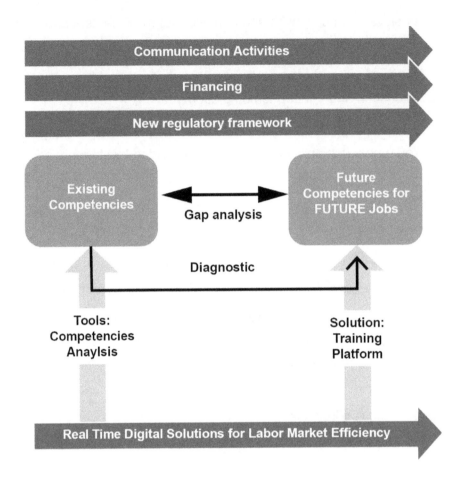

Figure 08: Key Components of the Toolbox

Chapter 6: Return on Investment

The financial reality experienced by governments and corporations alike provide all the rationale we need for upskilling. The cost of the growing talent shortage and competition for well-qualified staff – potentially causing salary increases – higher turnover of obsolete workers, the loss of revenue due to job vacancies, and the cost of unemployment, must all be considered when looking at talent recruitment and management expenses. Upskilling is a very effective way to mitigate these challenges. This chapter demonstrates that upskilling is the most effective solution when we use a realistic view of the financial costs to society.

The first section of this chapter presents options for corporations, governments and the workers to estimate upskilling return on investment (ROI). We discuss the merit of viewing upskilling initiatives as investments rather than as standard business or training expenses. We look at the components of this investment and include a wider, and more realistic definition of costs to benchmark and compare savings and gains. The second part of this chapter highlights different financial options that governments have used to accelerate upskilling investments in the economy.

The key is being able to demonstrate a healthy return on investment. Having the numbers and statistics that support the initiative enables CEOs and Ministers of Labour alike, to 'sell' the upskilling concept and engage key stakeholders. It can mean the difference between success and failure.

Upskilling ROI

In 2010, studies indicated that only 56% of EU-28 enterprises offered even the minimum of continuing vocational training (CVT).

Lack of time, no need for new skills and the cost of training were the most cited reasons. The paradigm shift needed, and the magnitude of financing required will triple training investment for each participating worker (on average €1356 per participant per capita). This is so important that a new technical and financial framework is required to unlock investments[89].

Upskilling is composed of different elements. Each one provides a unique view of the required investment and potential returns. Workforce planning exercises help define future skills and determine the number of employees who may need to work with new technology. As well as training and salary costs, an individual worker's skills and motivation must be assessed. Individual support during the upskilling process, using independent advisors, may be viewed as an added cost, but actually positively influences the initiative's success rate.

Examples of the Upskilling Investment Process

The examples in this chapter provide a concrete illustration of the value of using upskilling as the priority solution (compared to layoffs or new employee recruitment). We have calculated the return on investment (ROI) for corporations and governments with a very conservative assumption using profiles of low-skilled and high-skilled employees.

The first example uses John and Paul to illustrate the investment associated with an upskilling initiative. The variation in upskilling investment for these two cases (from €12,800 for John to €24,200 for Paul) reflects the higher salary and training investment for skilled employees.

To truly understand the potential for savings and other organisational benefits, we can examine two examples of upskilling investment decisions.

Engagement/Framework Assessment				
Upskilling Investment	John Low-skilled		Paul High-skilled	
	€	%	€	%
Monthly salary	**2,500**		**6,000**	
Corporate workforce planning (20% of salary)	500	4	1,200	5
Individual assessment and support Training: 320 hrs	2,500	20	3,000	12
2 months @ €15 & €25 respectively	4,800	38	8,000	33
Salary cost during training	5,000	39	12,000	50
Total	**12,800**	100	**24,200**	100

Table #04: Upskilling Assessment Elements

Example #1: Automation (Robotics) Layoffs

New robots will automate most of John and Paul's current tasks, making their jobs obsolete, but the company is recruiting new staff in other departments. Today, many managements would only consider the automation in the decision-making process. Corporate executives would consider laying off John and Paul without looking across the organisation for other options. Here the upskilling investment is benchmarked against lay-off costs.

Example #1: Upskill vs Layoffs		
Upskilling Investment	John Low-skilled	Paul High-skilled
Indemnity: 6 months' salary	€15,000	€36,000
Additional lay-off costs (legal, outplacement, training…) representing 3 & 6-months' salary respectively	€7,500	€36,000
Total layoff cost	**€22,500**	**€72,500**

Table #05: Upskill vs Layoffs

In practice, these lay-off costs are decidedly underestimated. Problems with unions or other social factors, including increased salary premium for new joiners (in the context of talent shortage) could also drive up costs. Indirectly, the company will also save on recruitment costs associated with filling future vacant positions that could easily be filled by internal staff. Depending upon country regulations, the sector, the social contracts in place and social climate, companies are offering up to 3 years of salary to laid-off workers. This alone, could amount to €90,000 for John and €216,000 for Paul.

By installing an upskilling programme, if John and Paul's skills profiles match the vacant jobs, the company stands to recoup a minimum of €9,700 for John (43% less than lay-off costs) and €47,800, for Paul (66% less than lay-off costs), without even considering any of the other many benefits of upskilling. Thus, upskilling is a clear solution to decrease unnecessary expenses and increase mobility.

Example #1: Upskilling ROI Summary		
	John Low-skilled	Paul High-skilled
Monthly salary	€2,500	€6,000
Upskilling investment	€12,800	€24,200
Minimum layoff cost estimation	€22,500	€72,000
Potential savings	**€9,700**	**€47,800**

Table #06: Upskilling ROI Summary

Compared to all the cases in Europe, this financial scenario is really very conservative in terms of savings. Of course, besides the financial benefit, the social, organisational and reputational gains from upskilling are far greater than laying off any workforce. This example does not calculate the potential State expense associated with the unemployed workers, or potential State investment in the upskilling initiative, which will clearly have an even more positive effect in terms of financial return.

Example 2: New Skills Not on the Market

The investment in new machines will require a full set of new skills and positions. The newly acquired machines have just been launched on the market, so very few people have experience working on them. In fact, there are essentially no workers available at all on the current job market. The company has created a new department, with two profiles that require very specific new generation machine expertise; an operator and a production line supervisor.

In the current decision-making process, executives first consider external recruitment via a recruitment agency. The focus is to hire workers and move them close to the factory. In this case, upskilling investment is benchmarked against revenue and marginal loss.

The position of the operator and the production line manager have been vacant for nine months, representing respectively a loss of revenues of €50,000 and €100,000. In addition, new recruits must be trained and on-boarded into the company. Jane and Pauline have been working in similar roles on older machines in another department. An upskilling investment of €12,800 for Jane and €22,500 for Pauline, will allow them to be operational in 3 months. The company would generate €50,000 and €100,000 in revenue with existing staff who have a low risk of failure because they are already integrated in the company. With a gross margin of 50%, the company would generate an additional margin of €12,200 for Jane and €27,500 for Pauline. It's true that the company would have to fill the vacant jobs left by Jane and Pauline, but it would be easier to upskill someone internally or even recruit externally for the skills required in the old jobs.

Therefore, upskilling investment provides a higher and more rapid gross margin than recruiting externally for jobs with difficult to fill skills profiles. In 6 months, the gross margin generated by the jobs' production, recovers the upskilling investment for the two profiles.

Example #2: Upskilling ROI Summary	Jane Low-skilled	Pauline High-skilled
Monthly salary	€2,500	€6,000
Upskilling investment	€12,800	€24,200
Average annual revenue generation	€100,000	€200,000
Gross margin (50%) on 6 months	€25,000	€50,000
Potential gross margin	€12,200	€25,800

Table #07: Upskilling ROI Summary

We have met with several manufacturers that are investing in Industry 4.0 technology, where the programme pivots on upskilling and increased internal mobility as the main job feed strategy. Their upskilling investment is clearly above €30,000 per capita and, in some cases, above €60,000. Their return on investment is still very high. These two examples are very practical cases, seen often in different sectors today. Upskilling investment provides a robust minimum savings of 43% against a lay-off scenario and is recovered in six months in the case of a talent shortage scenario.

Government Intervention

For governments, the potential ROI takes different forms. The financial impact of upskilling has a massive impact on GDP, public expenditures, tax revenues and labour ministry budgets that protect the unemployed. Here, we look at two key questions for the government.

- What is the impact of not supporting upskilling with public expenditures?

- What is the correct level of financial intervention to enable and accelerate upskilling?

The impact of not supporting upskilling with public expenditures

Let's take a look at the two examples from the government's perspective. In the first example, upskilling investment versus lay-off costs, the State would save unemployment costs estimated in 2012 to be between €19,000 in Spain up to €33,000 in Belgium[90].

Cross country overview of the average yearly cost of an unemployed worker (in Euro)						
Type of costs	Belgium	Germany	France	Spain	Sweden	UK
Public Intervention						
Unemployment benefits	€9,493	€8,793	€10,686	€10,778	€7,475	€3,561
Guidance & admin. costs	€1,683	€2,020	€1,641	€242	€3,018	€1,746
Total Public Intervention	**€11,176**	**€10,813**	**€12,327**	**€11,020**	**€10,493**	**€5,307**
Potential loss of revenue						
Loss in social contribution of employers	€8,747	€4,606	€10,172	€5,756	€8,585	€2,955
Loss in social contribution of workers	€4,104	€4,893	€3,294	€1,222	€1,911	€2,539
Loss of direct taxation	€8,240	€4,463	€1,888	€1,291	€2,489	€4,498
Loss of indirect taxation	€1,177	€776	€1,057	€700	€3,427	€2,710
Total Potential Loss of Revenue	**€22,267**	**€14,737**	**€16,411**	**€8,970**	**€16,412**	**€12,702**
Total average cost of an unemployed	**€33,443**	**€25,550**	**€28,737**	**€19,991**	**€26,905**	**€18,008**

Table #08: Average Yearly Cost of Unemployment

While the study from 2012 is quite old, the magnitude of these figures remains valid. This conservative estimate includes public support (unemployment benefits, etc.), and loss of government remittances (tax revenue, social contribution, etc.). In fact, the estimated loss to government revenue is higher than corporate upskilling costs. For our example to hold true, the employees must succeed in their new functions, and not need to draw upon unemployment benefits.

In the second scenario, in addition to direct revenue loss from the public budget, a vacant job represents a loss of gross domestic product growth for the State. The potential loss of revenue depends on individual taxation and social contribution and varies significantly from one country to another, so we will take a very conservative 20% rate of the individual revenue in our simulation below. While so many countries are looking for additional fractions of a percentage in growth, vacant jobs represent untapped potential.

Consider the impact caused by the serious lack of workers in the high-tech industry. In 2018, the European Photonics Industry Consortium (EPIC) posted 800 job offers from 167 companies across 47 countries[91]. This consortium promotes the development of organisations working in photonics, for example the production of semi-conductors, connected cars, etc. These 800 jobs represent an annual turnover loss of €160 million and a minimum public revenue loss of €32 million (20%). Given the limited number of graduates in this strategic field, the only current solution for corporations is to offer higher salaries to attract recruits from other photonics companies. An unsustainable strategy.

A €20 million photonic upskilling investment programme, targeting engineers and technicians from other industries suffering from high unemployment, would solve part of the problem and provide a very high return on investment in less than 12 months. A collaboration between regions with a strong photonics industry and EPIC could create and deploy an upskilling programme with the support of the EU and other governments. In both cases, upskilling would reduce public expenditures, prevent unemployment and accelerate the region's ability to fill vacant jobs.

Upskilling to Reduce Unemployment

In terms of the unemployed; upskilling would allow a portion of the unemployed to re-join the working population quite quickly. A complete and tailored upskilling programme would have a substantial impact on the community, business landscape and economy. It would provide unemployed workers with individualised professional advice and dedicated training to develop skills for targeted job requirements. This might be seen as a very complex solution, but the ROI is obvious.

According to the Court of Auditor's analysis, in 2016 France spent €5.6 billion to train unemployed workers, at an average cost of close to €1,600 per unemployed worker[92]. With an average success rate of 25% after six months, the current training programmes demonstrate very disappointing results, especially considering that 51% of trainees do not have a baccalaureate and therefore, fall into the highest 'at risk' population. This report calls for a full revamp of the system, as well as the assessment of job requirements, competencies, and training providers.

We created a small-scale coding school in France and Luxembourg with Brigitte Le Page (MD). 100 unemployed workers completed a 3-month upskilling programme. The government's investment was below €700,000. Graduates enjoyed a 70% placement rate in sustainable jobs, within 3 months of completing the programme. Based upon unemployment costs of €15,000 per person, the programme generated a 6-month savings of €800,000. Financially, there are clear benefits for governments to investigate the potential of upskilling in their region.

Return on Investment: Savings		
	John Low-skilled	Paul High-skilled
Government's annual spending for unemployment (averaged cost)	€25,000	€50,000
Upskilling investment	€12,800	€24,200
Average savings	€12,200	€26,200
Average additional revenue in 6 months (20% of annual salary)	€6,000	€7,200
Total savings and additional revenue	€18,200	€33,400
Time to recover full upskilling investment	8.5 months	8.7 months
Time to recover half of the upskilling investment	4.2 months	4.3 months

Table #09: Return on Investment: Savings

Add to these savings, the associated GDP gains and we see only two of the potential returns.

Return on Investment: GDP		
	John Low-skilled	Paul High-skilled
Government's annual loss of revenue in case of vacant job	€6,000 (20%)	€14,400 (20%)
Upskilling investment	€12,800	€24,200
Average additional revenue in 9 months with upskilling	€4,500	€10,800
Time to recover full upskilling investment	25.6 months	20.16 months
Time to recover half of the upskilling investment	12.8 months	10 months

Table #10: Return on Investment: GDP

Given the limited literature on the topic, governments and research centres should push for new studies into the economic impact of upskilling.

The Employee

Beyond corporations and government, the return on investment (ROI) for the individual employee is the most complex to assess. With upskilling, the employee will maintain or increase their revenue stream, thanks to a skills portfolio that is applicable to new jobs. However, this may not be attractive enough to mobilise the large majority of employees toward the massive investment of personal time required. The State and corporations must develop a reward system that materialises once the employee has successfully completed their upskilling. This reward could be a raise or bonus that is awarded upon successful completion of milestones. The development of this system must include appreciation that upskilling requirements are here to stay and many of the employees who undertake upskilling this year, will also require upskilling programmes within two to five years.

Corporations, the government and employees should be able to realise a clear financial gain through the launch of a large upskilling programme. To be sustainable, the initiative must be a three-way win. Given the numerous market imperfections and the current technological revolution, State objectives must include dedicating the right amount of budget, to most efficiently unlock private sector investment in upskilling. In a recent report on best practices in adapting skills to needs, the OECD recommendation was to '*Strengthen incentives for employers to invest in training to meet skill needs but minimise the administrative burden*' [93].

Reviewing programmes in different countries, shows that most are limited either in scope (training cost subsidy only), the magnitude of support (on average below €1,000 per employee), or the number or type of beneficiary (SMEs). Some support is also very burdensome and complex to obtain. However, we describe five cases (Canada, Belgium, Singapore, India, and Luxembourg) which provide a holistic approach for all employees and corporations; providing a significant amount of funding to meet the upskilling challenge.

Canada Job Grant (CJG)

Although somewhat controversial, this programme aims to ensure that current or potential employees are given the opportunity to improve their workplace skills. The underlying premise is that a trained workforce is more employable. The federal government subsidises two thirds of training cost for eligible workers, up to C$10,000, via each province. The employer pays the other third of the training cost and must apply for the government subsidy on behalf of the worker.

Recognised third-party organisations (either private or non-profit) must provide the training. In-house programmes are not eligible. The Canada Job Grant fund allocates just under $200 million annually and works in conjunction with other programmes such as job banks and alerts, youth employment strategies, aboriginal labour market and persons with disabilities programmes[94]. From a funding perspective, this aligns with the magnitude of funding required for upskilling, but it does not include proper corporate or individual skills assessment. Also, the $10,000 limit per grant may negatively influence upskilling in high-tech or Industry 4.0 manufactures.

Crédit Adaptation, Belgium

The Wallonia region in Belgium has implemented a dedicated grant for companies facing a structural, work organisation, or technological change, to upskill employees. The Crédit Adaptation programme amounts to €9 per training hour for small and medium-sized businesses (SMEs) and €6 per training hour for large companies. The overall amount is capped at €80,000 per company every two years. The region provides technical assistance that helps companies develop training plans. Main limitations include the very low hourly subsidy per employee training hour, the overall budget cap which limits this initiative to either being used by small companies (with few staff) or by fewer staff in the case of larger companies, and the lack of independent advice available to, and assessment required for, individuals[95].

SkillsFuture, Singapore

SkillsFuture brings together education and training providers, the government, employers and unions, in an effort to change the way the working population views learning and skills development. The national movement's objective is to provide organisations with the tools and support they need to upskill their workers within three to five years. The clarion call is giving all Singaporeans the opportunity to develop to their full potential, no matter their stage of life. The hope is that SkillsFuture will address the growing skills gap and drive Singaporeans towards a life-long learning model that supports and advances the economy and builds an inclusive society[96].

SkillsFuture provides full assistance to a variety of user groups: students, early career employees, mid-career employees, employers and training providers. The wide scope of technical assistance, started in 2016, includes career guidance, and individual training allowances of S$500 allocated to all potential and existing Singaporean workers aged 25 and over[97]. This encourages individuals to take ownership of their own skills development and lifelong learning plans. The government is responsible for periodic top-ups to the initial training credit which never expires. As well, individuals can apply for a SkillsFuture Study award, which provides $5,000 in financial assistance to 2,000 early-to mid-career Singaporeans, who wish to develop and deepen their skills in future growth clusters. The population can also access complementary programmes such as TechSkills Accelerator.

For employers, SkillsFuture provides technical assistance programmes and financing. Its main subsidy, to a maximum of S$15,000, can be used to offset the cost of structured training for employers of fresh polytechnic graduates. SkillsFuture has a rather generous additional funding programme for corporations suffering from talent shortages. In this scheme, between 50% and 90% of course fees are subsidised. The scheme clearly encourages companies to use certified courses and approved training providers through a cap of S$15 to S$25 per training hour for certified courses versus the $2 per hour for non-certified trainings.

Course Fee and Absentee Payroll Funding for Employers[98]				
Non-SMEs				
External Course Fee Funding				
Courses offered by SSG-appointed CET Centres	Non-PMET	Up to 90% of course fees	Up to 90% of course fees	Up to 95% of course fees
	PMET	Up to 70% of course fees	Up to 90% of course fees	
Certifiable courses approved by SSG	Non-PMET	80% of course fees capped at $17/hour	90% of course fees capped at $25/hour	
	PMET	50% of course fees capped at $15/hour	90% of course fees capped at $50/hour	
Non-certifiable	Non-PMET & PMET	$2/hour		

Table #11: Fees/Absentee Payroll Funding[98]

source: SSG.gov.sg

Overall, Singapore has one of the most supportive upskilling programmes in the world. It provides complete and well-thought-through assistance at all levels.

India – National Skill Development Cooperation[99]

The National Skill Development Corporation in India (NSDC), established in 2009, is a not-for-profit set up by the Ministry of Finance. The Government of India, through the Ministry of Skill Development & Entrepreneurship (MSDE) holds 49%, while the private sector has a 51% share. NSDC's mission is to promote skills development and re-skilling in labour market entrants (15 to 59 years old) through funding short-term skills development programmes. With a horizon of 3- to 12-months and courses that take up to 600 hours, this initiative provides placement and special focus on entrepreneurial opportunities for women.

It supports scalable and profitable quality vocational training initiatives run by large, for-profit institutions and is expected to help fill the 109 million job vacancies in 24 key sectors that are projected to have workforce gaps by 2022. It will also employ about 15,000 trainers, 3,000 assessors, boost GDP and transform the country into a competitive middle-income economy, by skilling up 8.8 million workers. This World Bank initiative, injected $250 million into the SIMO (Skills India Mission Operation) project and focuses on quality assurance, information systems, and train-the-trainer academies. It provides funding directly or via partnerships to skills training providers. This supports high-quality training and vocational systems to upskill Indian workers, while sparking the development of appropriate models to enhance and coordinate initiatives in 21 private sectors.

Skills Asset Managers & National Agencies

Involving international development banks in initiatives such as these improves the quality of governance, forces national stakeholders to track results and measure real impact. As well as interim achievements, the World Bank's public report measures 15 risks. Projects and programmes such as this, stimulate private initiatives and the emergence of a new type of asset manager – the Skills Asset Manager.

Upskill capital, is a new impact investor in India[100]. It launched a pilot project to fund, in collaboration with a non-profit organisation, new innovative vocational and employability skills training, and career guidance for young people from disadvantaged communities. The fund pays the tuition fees of 400 students and recovers the costs as a portion of their wages once they are employed. It is easy to see the importance of creating a National Skills Development Agency, complemented by a full eco-system of non-profit and for-profit organisations. Operational investments for the Skill India Mission demonstrates the need to mobilise development capital for upskilling projects.

Luxembourg Skills Bridge

The Luxembourg Skills Bridge initiative is open to any companies facing a major shift in their work organisation due to technological and digital investments. It takes an anticipative approach to improving workforce employability. The financial support provided by this programme differs from any other initiative in the country. What sets it apart is the company- and individual-level support and the coverage afforded via technical assistance (up to 80% of training costs without any limit, with an additional 90% salary compensation during the training period). The initiative is designed around limiting the programme's administrative burden for the participating companies and reinforces company workforce planning practices. Highlights of technical and financial assistance are detailed in the chart on opposite page.

In terms of government sponsorship, we clearly see the difference between a larger, holistic approach that includes technical assistance support and those with limited scope that only partially cover training costs.

Proposed Technical & Financial Assistance	
Support for employee	Financial support the company receives
Technical assistance for workforce planning & employee assessment	Maximum 12 days per company
Individual coaching through pilot	1 day per employee
Training cost per employee (reimbursement on invoices)	Internal mobility: 35%
	External mobility, same sector: 50%
	External mobility, different sector: 80%
Salary cost during training ("chomage partiel")	90% of employee's salary, limited to a maximum of 250% of the minimum wage

Table #12: Technical and Financial Assistance Proposed

From Subsidies to Performance Fee Models

Given the high number of vacant IT and tech-related positions on the job market, quality training providers that offer tailored programmes should be entitled to at least partially participate in a scheme that affords higher remuneration potential. We believe that the government should support training costs via a success fee model. Measures would be tied to the successful placement of upskilled worker in a new job.

This success fee model transforms the economic landscape into a demand-driven market, significantly reducing the financial risk for public expenditure and also increasing the return on investment for corporations and workers. The major advantage of this new business model is in aligning all stakeholders involved in the upskill process, towards the same achievement measure; the successful on-boarding of the upskilled worker into a new job.

Main Messages

It is clear that upskilling initiatives afford a superb ROI for corporations, individuals and most of all the government. Given the complexity and volume of investments required, we recommend that governments review their intervention schemes and focus on a holistic approach. A significant amount of support, a strong methodology, coupled with a minimum of 50% coverage of overall costs, ensures the success of upskilling interventions over the long-term, and that a country's workforce is truly employable. Building an upskilling ecosystem that includes important dimensions; regulations, workforce planning, individual skills assessment, role model employers and employees, as well as streamlined upskilling administration, massively contributes to the overall success of a national or regional upskilling initiative.

Upskilling is a clear demonstration of long-term trust between company management and their people. Management trusts people to execute their new strategy through the acquisition of new skills. Employees can rest assured that they will not become obsolete while they participate in regular upskilling initiatives. The positive impact is wide-spread …

For the corporation:

- Well-qualified, motivated staff, ready to take on new jobs and be part of the thriving organisation

- Available skilled local talent pool

- Lower staff turnover and cost savings in recruitment, salary and workforce management (including layoff indemnities, outplacement, etc.)

- A high-performing HR department, aligned with the company's business strategy

- Positive community brand association (CSR impact)

- Higher revenue (fewer vacant positions, filled more quickly)

For the individual:

- Increased revenue stream (better pay as workers progress to higher-skilled jobs)

- Ability to re-join the workforce in productive jobs

- Professional advice regarding job mobility, career options and planning

- Increased job satisfaction

For governments:

- Increased tax revenue (increased number of workers)

- Healthy GDP growth (lower unemployment)

- Lower public expenditures (unemployment benefits, etc.)

- Improved upskilling policies and regulations that support enriched employment

- Positive country brand association for international corporations looking for locations with highly skilled populations

- Well-qualified, motivated workers, for a thriving digital economy

- Accelerating economy sparked by full employability of workers

There are many examples of successful upskilling initiatives around the world that confirm the beneficial ROI – both in monetary rewards and well-being for the individual, society and business. The challenge is to design an upskilling scheme that provides maximum and measurable impact for the specific region or business sector.

Chapter 7: Financing Solutions

In the last section, we demonstrate the high return on investment for corporations and the high level of savings and additional revenue that governments can realise in less than a year. We estimate that on an annual basis, a country must invest around €1 billion per tranche of 100,000 low-skilled employees, and €2 billion per tranche of high-skilled employees.

With a working population of 246 million in Europe, this means that upskilling a mere 5% of the population (12 million people a year - 6 million low-skilled and 6 million high-skilled) requires €220 billion in funding. The equivalent of 1.5% of the EU's GDP (€15,300 billion in 2017)[101]. The ROI is at least double this expenditure. At approximately €500 billion, it is the equivalent of 3% of the EU's GDP.

This financial opportunity leaves room for mobilising third-party financing. We can identify three main sources and vehicles: debt, insurance and investment. This chapter provides an analysis of different financing solutions and provides a financial tool box for CEOs. This chapter, especially, demonstrates that investment in the workforce skills portfolio can become a significant asset class, included in evaluations and financial health reviews by investors.

Enabling Success

For most upskilling initiatives to realise their potential, the government must support enabling financial conditions via national policy review/revision that reduce barriers to participation. For corporations, SMEs and workers, these policy revisions will help accelerate upskilling investment. Governments alone will not solve this financial challenge. Insurers, bankers, and impact investors all have key roles to play in designing solutions for this new intangible class of investment. The key priority for executives must be finding free or cheap money to finance upskilling initiatives and optimise cash management. This could be quite a large untapped market for financial institutions.

Debt, Loan or Upskilling Impact Bond

For governments, access to new debts is a possibility but does not necessarily fit the model directly. However, access to special investment loans, granted by international development banks such as the European Investment Bank, or the Asian Infrastructure Bank are all viable options. The exciting aspect of many upskilling programmes is their ability to demonstrate ROI. Because the numbers hold true in virtually every circumstance, governments are free to create a contribution mix between national and third-party investors. This gives a few interesting options, not only for the State to support upskilling initiatives, but for organisations to realise opportunities associated with upskilling for the future. The examples that follow are just a few of the possible financing mixes using currently available vehicles.

State and Development Bank Loans

This is an interesting support mechanism. The country finances 50% of the effort on its own and obtains the other 50% through international development bank loans. Managed as a loan portfolio by the State, upskilling financing could be granted to successful corporate applicants. This loan portfolio approach can be used for a specific project or as a key strategic element of national industrial investment plans. Through State upskilling loan portfolio schemes, companies can obtain financing for both upskilling their workers and new machine purchases together.

Payments Tied to Results

An even more innovative option is to issue social bonds for upskilling certain segments or categories of workers. This is an emerging solution that is very interesting from the perspective of governance and risk-sharing between private and public stakeholders but is rather limited in size. An illustration of this solution is the Finnish company, Epiqus, which is responsible for operating Social Impact bond, Koto-SIB; supporting migrant and refugee integration in Finland[102]. The European Investment Fund invested €10 million in this scheme designed with the Ministry of Economic Affairs and Employment of Finland and Epiqus, and has a specialist fund manager dedicated to impact investing[103]. With this social impact bond trial, the EIF and the Finnish government aim to provide education and upskilling to 2,500 to 3,700 migrants. That translates into an investment of between €2,702 and €4,000 for each participant. This is a very modest amount compared to the potential savings in terms of refugee and immigrant population support. It also accelerates integration and provides other benefit to society and the economy.

The distinctive feature of impact investing is their focus on outcomes. The remuneration of the fund is directly linked to the success of the upskilling programme. Epiqus acts as a regulated intermediary; a fund manager between investors, service providers and beneficiaries of the programme. It gathers private and public investment on agreed objectives and organises procurement and operations to deliver the results successfully.

The fund manager holds full responsibility for the programme. The investment firm defines the specifications for training programmes and uses open calls to obtain tenders for the best solutions on the market. In the case of migrant integration, success is defined as fast- track integration training and employment of 2,500 migrants in three years. Payment-for-results schemes provide some level of remuneration to all investors (fund managers, social organisations and training providers) but the amount is dependent upon the successful placement of the migrant or refugee in a job. The government tracks all results, including economic and social revenues, which are audited by a third party.

According to the Ministry of Economic Affairs, Labour and Employment, 'Rapid employment of immigrants reduces integration training costs, employment benefit pay-outs and increases tax collection.' On average, this scheme saves public funds while improving the sustainability of business and industry in the region/country. This innovative example demonstrates that payment-by-results schemes can successfully upskill and integrate vulnerable populations into the labour market. There is no reason why the same approach would not work, perhaps even more effectively, for the existing, employed workforce in companies that are already integrated. The only appreciable difference is that the scheme might be organised in a slightly different manner (see State and Development Bank Loans above) and might not be considered as a purely social impact bond (SIB) structure, but more as an upskilling impact bond (UIB).

The consolidation of tangible and intangible requirements into a solid investment case facilitates understanding and acceptance by bankers. Investing in new machines without investing in the right skills to operate them should, of course, always be considered a major risk factor that increases the chance of failure exponentially.

Positive Outlook for Upskilling Impact Investment

Investing in upskilling is still in its infancy but fits very well with impact investing. Over the last ten years, impact investors, with the objective to positively influence social and environmental areas, along with netting out a financial return, have increased investments in education. However, according to the last Global Impact Investment Network survey, 41% of impact investor respondents allocate investment to education. This represents only 4% of $228 billion assets under management[105]. Less than $10 billion is allocated to this critical area. The report also highlights that 82% of impact investors surveyed, indicate that investment returns are in line with expected impact and financial performance.

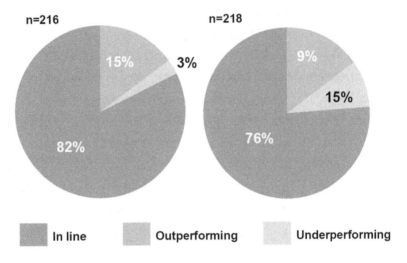

N= Number of respondents; some respondents chose 'not sure' and are not included

Figure #09: Performance Relative to Expectations
Source: GINN

Currently, impact investors focus mainly on basic education for poor and disadvantaged populations in developing regions and emerging markets.

Sector Allocations by AUM

Percent of AUM, n=226; total AUM = USD 228.1 billion

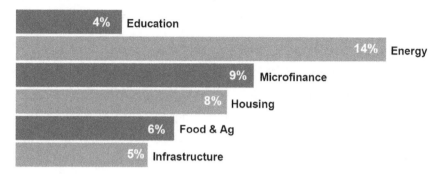

4%	Education
14%	Energy
9%	Microfinance
8%	Housing
6%	Food & Ag
5%	Infrastructure

Figure #10 Sector Allocation by AUM
Source: GINN

The European Investment Bank initiated innovative financing products to support investments in industry and education. In 2017, the EIB supported educational projects with €2.5 billion. Given the ambition of the Juncker Plan, with a €315 billion investment target, there is a significant opportunity for upskilling ventures if governments, banks and corporations understand the urgency and the scale of the required investment.

Corporate Upskilling Investment

In January 2018, Walt Disney announced the launch of an investment programme specifically designed to cover tuition costs for hourly employees. The initial budget of $50 million supports new and ongoing education and vocational training, with a further annual injection of up to $25 million[104]. The concept is outstanding; it puts employees in the driver's seat to manage meaningful and productive work lives. For the 88,000 eligible employees, this programme allows them to engage in work-specific training or education aimed at skilling themselves up for their next, potential position. It impacts their ability to control elements related to their career aspirations and to advance. This initiative is one of the first of this scale. It paves the way for future corporate upskilling practices. For this type of scheme, corporations could invest their own assets but could also trigger or leverage third party assets.

Investment in workforce upskilling is just beginning. Together, basic education and workforce upskilling investments amount to trillions. Upskilling is about widening the economic and social opportunity for everyone ... during their total career lifecycle. New players, new governance, new approaches are all needed for this concept to be a success.

Debt Instruments

Most impact investors look only at market return rates. Developed Markets (DM) have a lower return than Emerging Markets (EM) with a higher standard deviation, the large majority fail to reach their market rate target. With impact investors looking for a return rate that is below market, on average, DM investors realise a higher return rate than expected. Most investors with a market rate objective of 4% against 1.9%, will see EMs overperform DMs (6.1% against 4%). All realised returns are below the initial 7% target rate, which is the minimum refinancing cost for financial institutions on the debt market.

Equity

Market rate investors gain a double-digit return while below market rate investors realise performance of 7 to 8.4%. The figure below shows the average gross return since inception of the fund.

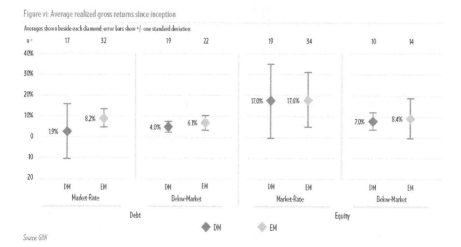

Figure vi: Average realized gross returns since inception

Averages shown beside each diamond; error bars show +/- one standard deviation.

Source: GIIN

Figure #11: Debt vs Equity Performance

Building Risk-Adjusted Market Returns

The large amount of potential savings and additional revenue, for corporations and governments alike, leaves room for targeted market rate return through equity or debt instruments. We have built up different models and scenarios to assess the risk profile of an upskilling impact investment. We analysed an upskilling programme based upon 100 people with:

Scenario 1: a 70% success rate in placing upskilling participants in new jobs within three months of graduation (with 30% not placed in jobs within the first six months)

Scenario 2: a 50% success rate in placing upskilling participants in new jobs (and 50% not placed)

Scenario 3: a success rate of placing 30% of upskilling participants in new jobs (and 70% not placed)

The hypothesis produces the following data:

Scenario Data Assumptions	
Data input	
Cost of upskilling programme	€30,000/person
Layoff cost	€80,000/person
Cost for the State	€80,000/person
Total cost of the programme if not successsful	€190,000/person
% of investors renumeration on savings	10%/person
Payment split for the company	50%/person
Payment split for the State	50%/person
Volatility of the upskilling programme success	7%/person

Table # 13: Scenario Data Assumptions

Simulation Factors:

- 100 people in the programme

- €30,000 is paid by the investor for each participant from Day-1 (€3 million)

- 1,000 simulations for each scenario

- No behavioural differences between people (tool ready but not used at this stage)

- Volatility used to hit the "trigger" (eg 'Failure of the programme' has been calibrated by trial and error, no observations exist)

- Default of payment has not been considered in these simulations (eg no reimbursement from companies to the 'fund' that provides pre-financing for the programme)

- Default of upskilling programme sponsors' payment (generally a government) has not been considered as an option in the simulations

The following results were obtained for each scenario.

Scenario 1: With a 70% success rate, including 30% failure rate costs, investors with a contracted 10% savings on potential layoff costs would gain, on average, €827,390 (eg a global return rate of 27% on the programme). The savings for the State added to the savings for the company would be shared equally at €3.7 million.

Scenario 2: With a success/failure rate of 50%, investors with a contracted 10% saving on potential layoff costs would gain on average €502,949 (eg a global return rate of 17% on the programme). The savings for the State and company would be equally shared at €2.2 million.

Scenario 3: With a success/failure rate of 30%/70%, investors with a contracted 10% of savings on potential layoff costs would gain on average €179,310 (eg a global return rate of 6% on the programme). The savings for the State and the company would be equally shared at €806,898.

These simulations demonstrate the potential return of an upskilling programme against layoff cost only. They are mainly influenced by the upskilling participants' placement success rate, by the risk profiles of the region, and companies and people participating in the initiative.

Reducing the risk profile of an upskilling programme is fundamental in obtaining investor commitment. A high-risk situation dissuades any investor from participating. The investor looks at the risk/remuneration ratio, which must be favorable enough to entice them to invest. The risk profile of an upskilling programme can be controlled effectively by implementing the following measures:

-   Develop a feasibility study and highlight the enablers as well as barriers of the environment

- Link the upskilling programme clearly to sizeable and sustainable job opportunities, for example, IT or professional services

- Implement a robust and proven upskilling methodology and tools that enhance in-depth corporate and individual assessments

- Precisely defined new training requirements, including horizontal, vertical and digital skills and select providers with a proven track record

- Define an operating model driven by the successful placement of upskilling participants, in which the different stakeholders align

- Get a guarantee or first loss mechanism from a government or a development bank to de-risk at least a part of the project for investors

Skills Insurance

Insurance solutions are also a very interesting future opportunity. From a policy perspective, establishing a regulatory framework that would make an individual skills insurance plan available from the first day of a citizen's career and run all the way to their retirement, is a very innovative solution. Financed jointly by the employee and employer, it allows specific tax benefits and provides a significant pool of funding to enable massive upskilling when needed during the individual's career.

This two-pronged approach would also encourage the employee and employer to share responsibility for employability and for keeping the skills portfolio current. As well as guaranteeing funds to regularly upskilling the working population, it allows clear conversations about the responsibility to upskill. The funds are administered by fund managers who would remain at arms-length;

facilitating the employee's external mobility, independently from company assets.

In France, the government implemented individual training accounts that include individual skills plan modules. An initial credit of €500 per employee, is capped at €5,000 per worker[115]. Companies are encouraged to make additional contributions in cases where the total amount available is not sufficient to fully finance training cost. For the low-skilled workforce, amounts were raised to €800 (initial credit) with a €8,000 ceiling. Employee assistance is reinforced with individual skills assessment and professional guidance. This interesting reform mobilises and aligns social partners, corporations and employees.

From the company's perspective, the insurance solution provides a two-fold benefit. First, if regulatory frameworks enable companies to consider human capital as the main asset, organisations could develop their own skills insurance plan. This type of plan sets aside savings that are directed toward longer periods of study, and secures funds in case of disability, illness or death, as a method of periodisation. The ideal case is when the regulatory framework enables the employee, as well as the company, to accumulate tax benefits against a small portion of an annual salary. Through a system of deductible skill insurance premiums, social contributions and taxes would be reduced for the individual and the company. The organisation is compelled to offer high-quality individual support and training that helps employees select sustainable career paths. This requires a new generation of HR professional, with higher capacity for strategic forecasting. The success criteria for an insurance-based plan includes:

- Enabling regulatory environment
- Full leadership commitment to developing a long-term, human capital and skills strategy

- Higher capacity human resources department
- Communications regarding tangible advantages; laid out clearly for the employee

The second way to implement this solution is to use an insurance company product. Unfortunately, private insurance companies have not yet developed mainstream skills insurance premiums. The absence of market demand, data, records of accomplishment, regulatory framework barriers and the general lack of innovation seen in most insurance companies, are some of the reasons for this gap in the market. Given the increasing importance of intangible assets, and CEOs' growing interest in this topic, we are sure that in the relatively near future, some insurer is bound to launch a product that enables companies to manage upskilling investments, especially in cases where there are large-scale technological changes.

The key challenge for insurers is assessing the probability of an event and defining it properly. We have discussed this scheme with some European insurers and they seem quite interested in investigating this new market opportunity. Large-scale pilot projects in Finland, Luxembourg or Singapore would be very useful to provide the detailed data required by insurers. The advanced mobilisation of pension funds is a very interesting solution as well. The widespread application of this type of scheme envisions higher volumes of financing through advanced mobilisation of collective or individual pension funds. This approach would be more market-driven and led by corporations. It raises many social, financial and societal questions, but it could be quite a creative element in the upskilling financing equation.

Skills Asset Managers

The Skills Asset Manager is already in place for Epiqus, UpSkill Capital and SkillsFuture. These organisations are a natural evolution of training associations. The American Society for Training & Development (now the Association for Talent Development), for example, started as a loose network of training professionals. This not-for-profit is now the clearing house for the most polished and expert training professionals on the globe. The Skills Assets Manager takes the training association concept to the next level by not only vetting training companies but by providing a results-based framework that allows government, business and individual trainees to have confidence in the system.

Much more than a traditional fund manager regulated by the financial authorities, social impact bond investment organisations have an additional layer of matching money to high-quality training provision. Their responsibility is far broader, but their role today is not well-known. There is quite an opportunity for governments to work with stakeholders to create an appropriate framework for developing Skills Asset Manager activities.

We already see this happening in a number of different constituencies. Instructus, based in the UK, the largest authority for apprenticeship programmes, sets standards and promotes education and learning for public benefit. The Pari Centre for New Learning partnered with six other organisations to realise the UniGrowCity project, aimed to tie adult learning to experienced-based learning regarding the future of sustainable cities.

The Expected Return on Investment

Beyond employment impact, asset managers and their investors look for a financial return of their investments. The analysis of impact investors' gross return realised since the inception of the fund provides very interesting insights with regard to ROI on upskilling impact investment. According to the Global Impact Investing Network (GIIN) report, 64% of surveyed investors look for market-rates that are risk-adjusted and 36% look for returns that are below market rates, this is quite a significant majority of the impact investor group[107].

n=229

	64%	Risk adjusted, market-rate returns
	20%	Below-market-rate returns: closer to market rate
	16%	Below-market-rate returns: closer to capital preservation

Source: GINN

Figure 12: Impact Investors Target Financial Returns

Main Messages

In reality, trillions are needed to upskill the global workforce on a continuous basis. Mobilising the private sector, including pension funds, is essential. Defining clear incentives and de-risking measures will grow investment in upskilling initiatives. The design of an innovative regulatory framework for upskilling investment funds is an interesting tactic with the emerging role of an upskilling asset manager.

Insurance is a very promising area for providing future solutions. It holds clear advantages for all stakeholders. Again, policy makers must enable this market innovation by providing a better regulatory framework, stimulating new research and launching pilot projects to generate relevant datasets that can be used to build innovative skills insurance products. The opportunity for impact investors in upskilling programmes is huge and presents a very attractive profile. As an emerging asset class, the lack of data about different markets and sectors limit short-term growth, but the presence of third-party investors can improve the quality of governance and the measurement of impacts. We would recommend that governments launch projects involving impact investors as observers to familiarise them with the approach and to accelerate the investment flow.

Section III:
Upskilling Ecosystem Paradigm Shift

KEY CONCEPTS

Individuals
- Need to bolster entrepreneurial capabilities in Europe
- Upskilling allows workers to truly engage & care for their future
- New skills portfolio for individuals: From T-Shaped to H-Shaped skills model

Government
- Jobs do not remain in the same location forever if a skilled workforce is not available
- Multiply by 10 the investment in upskilling: we must view the workforce as a massive component of investment/return
- Enable the worker to be more responsible for skills portfolio, through a national framework tied to a corporate strategy
- Upskill civil servants within a new career framework. New educational priorities

Organisations
- Which competencies tomorrow?
- Upskilling workers for a job-to-job transition is possible and sustainable
- New Corporate HR strategy & organisation required to develop high value workforce skills planning
- From Industry 4.0 to HR 5.0

Chapter 8: Upskilling Paradigm Shift

This chapter delves further into our thinking on the current crisis and examines solutions that are already beginning to emerge. We hope it provides insight into options for executing the 6-Step Solution to Upskilling and illustrates the importance of positioning upskilling initiatives correctly to net out the largest gains and to minimise barriers to success.

Competencies and Jobs Types

Most of the current workforce was educated between 1970 and 2000 during a time when most technologies, ubiquitous today, did not exist. The internet too, was in its infancy. From 1970 to 2000, most educational systems provided students with a solid foundation of basic knowledge and did not necessarily focus on teaching students how to learn. It was assumed that students would be able to easily acquire new skills via vocational or on-the-job training in the future. The skills model was one-dimensional: develop a very thorough vertical expertise with some good commercial skills. A degree was enough to put just about anyone on a good career path.

Between 2000 and 2012, the soft skills training industry emerged as it became obvious that these skills were integral to success in the new business landscape. Communicating with impact, team work, leadership, team management and innovation started to appear as themes in corporate training programmes.

When the economic crisis hit (2008), entrepreneurship and innovation quickly became a prominent focus. Many studies began to highlight the lack of entrepreneurship within European countries compared to USA. In 2003, the Global Entrepreneurship Monitor

(GEM), indicated that entrepreneurship in European countries landed between 4% (France) and 6% (Germany), while in the USA 12% of the adult population was involved in entrepreneurial activities. Economic and social context, and the individuals' capabilities and perceived opportunities contribute to the differences between countries. In 2011, Germany (37%) and France (38%) had significantly less of their population with the required entrepreneurial capabilities that the 56% in the US, or the 41% global average[108]. According to the latest 2017 report, the situation has not improved, with Europe remaining quite weak overall in terms of perceived entrepreneurship capabilities[109]. Organisations are beginning to realise that they require more entrepreneurial and soft skills within their ranks to ensure robust corporate development. This is one of the areas which requires significant upskilling.

Our description of upskilling also includes predicting and defining clear job targets and tailoring training to allow workers to enter desirable job categories. The purpose of upskilling employees whether corporate or government, is to create and maintain sustainable jobs, which generate growth and revenues through new transversal, digital and vertical skills. The 2018 PwC global CEO survey reveals that 91% of CEOs feel the need to strengthen their organisations' soft skills to compliment digital skills. Still, more than three quarters (76%) are concerned with the lack of digital skills in their workforce. As well, some CEOs are *extremely* concerned (22%) with digital skills in their own workforce; while 23% are extremely concerned that their leadership teams also lack digital skills. This indicates a significant business threat[3].

From 2012 to 2018, the digital transformation of the global economy expanded quickly. More and more, high-tech skills are required by industry. The BSA foundation report evidences the creation of more than 10 million jobs in the software industry[110]. Rising Above the Gathering Storm indicates that 85% of measured per capita income growth in the USA was due to technological change over a period of more than 100 years[111]. In Europe, most technology companies face a massive challenge to fill their vacant positions. The demand for high-tech skills is on a solid growth track. The EU28 is projected to have 8.7 million IT practitioners by 2020[112]. The latest (January 2017) EU Commission estimate pegs the gap between demand and supply at 500,000 in 2020[113].

All segments of the company (HR executives, management and employees) must be able to work together to anticipate and correctly predict future skills gap[111]. It is already too late if organisations wait until workers cannot meet specific job requirements or are unable to perform using the required technology. Manufacturing companies buying new lines of robots to replace semi-automated production lines, must consider upskilling during the investment decision phase, not after the purchase is complete. It is incumbent upon the organisation to treat upskilling as a major and critical component of the upgrades programme. Key topics must be…

- which workers will be impacted by this new investment?

- who will, or won't, be capable of managing the new machines?

- what skill gaps will be created and how it can be closed?

- what types of jobs will be available for those who are motivated and qualified, but whose skills are not aligned with new job requirements?

In a time where well-developed soft skills are becoming the rule not the exception, organisations must demonstrate those skills as well. Management must plan for discussions and interaction with individuals and groups as the essential job skills matching process takes place. It must demonstrate its high regard for the company's population, for its know-how and its knowledge.

Clear Job Targets: Today and for Tomorrow

As mentioned, upskilling is about an individual acquiring a specific competence to deliver a new task successfully. Upskilling requires that new tasks be defined and described precisely. Upskilling for a new or modified job varies radically from the generic, high-level training programme which provides non-specific knowledge.

Example: JAVA

As an example, consider the situation where there is high market demand for JAVA programmers in Europe. One company has tried, unsuccessfully, to recruit well-qualified JAVA programmers. A young programmer, not an engineer, who already works for this company, has independently started some online courses to learn JAVA but has not yet acquired the foundational knowledge and skills needed to fill the position. Through an investigation of this person's motivation and interests, the HR team would flag the worker, and offer them the job, contingent upon their successful completion of upskilling via their current training programme.

Traditionally, the minimum requirement to gain a solid foundation in JAVA would be approximately 800 hours, spread over close to two years of university study. As an online course, the worker can progress at their own speed, accelerating the learning curve. By supporting their worker in achieving this learning goal, the organisation signals that proactivity and commitment to life-long learning is rewarded. It shows employees that the organisation, itself, accepts alternate forms of education – sending a message to the population to consider all their learning and development options.

Example: Luxembourg

Another example is a case from 2007. The Luxembourg investment industry was desperately looking for hundreds of fund accountants. An entrepreneur partnered with an industry association

and a local employment agency. It offered to search for unemployed, recent graduates such as chemical engineers or statisti-
cians, and to provide an intense, 3-month training course for fund
accounting. This would allow participants to assume the new job
almost immediately. The programme was very effective; training
and placing more than 50 people in positions within months. This
was a giant success story for the industry and promoted rapid upskilling. With the right motivation and collaborative mind-set, much
can be accomplished very quickly.

These two examples illustrate the importance of timing in the
upskilling process, and the value of taking a 'sustainable jobs'
perspective. It also illustrates the significant impact of purposeful,
quality training design. But complications can arise because it
is not just up to the corporations; employees must be motivated
enough to buy into the concept of re-skilling. They must be willing
to invest their own time and effort into the new intense training
method. The upskilling process is a strategic decision that requires
6- to 12-months of employee training *and* concentrated management support, including planning and implementation of upskilling
initiatives. It only works if management and employees work together to forecast and anticipated gaps and create a flexible plan
to fill them.

Purposeful Training Designed to Fit the Job

Upskilling is highly specialised and customised training designed
to fit clearly defined job specifications. Whether it is designed
by the company or a third party, it encompasses the machines,
software, tech and soft skills involved in the work. Each module
has clear skills acquisition objectives and milestones but works on
a condensed timeframe. This abbreviated interval is critical to success, as the trainee either continues to perform their current job or
is only replaced on a short-term basis while in the programme.

The accelerated timetable is also fundamental to keeping participants' buy-in high, as well as motivating and helping them stay on course during the programme. Generally, a company can support an employee's absence for a maximum of three months, during the full-time upskilling training. This covers approximately 500 hours (40 hours of training per week) – the equivalent of one year of university study. The upskilling structure can also be designed to cover a longer period, allowing more balance between work and training hours. For example, a large airplane manufacturer has recently trained 500 employees as data analysts, using a 200-hour programme that stretched over 12 weeks.

Which Competencies Tomorrow?

Competency models have been used for decades to illustrate the skills required to survive and thrive in a variety of positions and work environments. From I- to T- to H- or X-shaped models, the list is practically infinite[114]. We are concentrating on a few that seems most able to express the needs of the working population going forward. The I-shaped model from the mid-20th century, was based only on acquiring vertical (in-depth) skills for one job, in one single area. The T-shaped skills model was first described in 1991 by David Guest and then further developed by different firms and institutions. While the vertical bar represents the depth of skills and expertise related to a single area or profession, the horizontal represents the extent of transversal skills required, for example, the ability to communicate and collaborate effectively across disciplines.

Overall, a wide horizontal bar on the T, indicates a person who is able to master different disciplines and systems and adapt rapidly to constant evolutions in job/skills requirements.

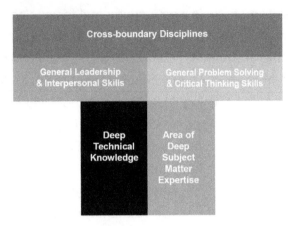

Figure #13: T-shaped Skills Model

Boundary crossing competencies require empathy, curiousness, and enthusiasm; characteristics which allow people to imagine a problem from different perspectives, engage with other stake-holders, and to design meaningful solutions. Positive outcomes include faster problem-solving processes, higher levels of innova-tion, and more deeply-shared corporate culture and vision. But is the T-shaped model adequate for this new era? M, K, and X have appeared as new symbolic letters for multi-shaped skills models. These new models focus on increasing one's capacity to evolve and master additional disciplines or transferable skills. Overall, these qualities have emerged as most in-demand for the market today. However, we would like to advance a more human dimen-sion for a world invaded by technology. We prefer an H-Shaped model.

The first vertical focuses on a deep set of technical expertise. The second vertical focuses on the increasing need for digital expertise in almost every job. The transversal bar links the technical and the digital elements and focuses on skills such as the ability to com-municate and collaborate effectively across disciplines, but also comprises the individual's capacity for enhanced and accelerated learning.

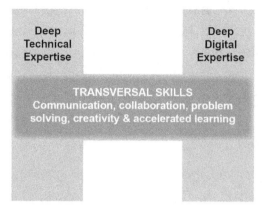

Figure 14: H-shaped Skills Model

Going forward, the ability to learn faster and smarter, will be one of the most important skills required by corporations. The H- or Human-Shaped model aims to keep the individual at the heart of all activities and concentrates corporate investments, as well as public policies, on the success of regularly upskilling the worker. It acknowledges that there is clear advantage to engaging in open dialogue which facilitates buy-in and collaboration between different stakeholders.

Example: Irish National Skills Strategy

The Irish Minister for Education and Skills, M. Bruton, encapsulated and expressed the paradigm shift for governments well,

> *"Our aim must be to improve the matching of the skills and needs across the board. We must focus on providing opportunities at all stages in life to all people to improve and expand their skills or change direction in their careers. We must also provide different pathways for people to reach their full potential."[115]*

Ireland's <u>National Skills Strategy 2025</u> has a core objective to double the amount invested in upskilling (from €543 to €1,300 per employee) by 2025[116]. The Minister for Education and Skills translates the current challenge into a simple, understandable statement, "winning the war for talent can be achieved by ensuring that all of Ireland's citizens have access to the skills they need to succeed in life; and Irish business has the people with the skills they need to grow."

Although simply phrased, this is much more of a challenge from an investment perspective. The average increase of €1,300 for each employee, is ten times less than is needed to upskill workers to the level required by most industries. The way to effectively maintain employability is to change the model. To upskill at least 10% of the population at any given time. The paradigm shift for all governments is to increase their investment in education and vocational training – from the first years of school to the end of one's career. The current learning model, which concentrates on the first 25 years of people's lives, is over. Workers need continuous learning throughout their careers. This fits with workers' opportunities for taking career breaks as most will be compelled to work longer. How much should the State, a corporation or an individual invest? These are very complex questions which require a toolbox of options to fit different purposes and situations.

Example: Swedish Wood Industry Case

Another huge influence in this area is the challenge of immigration and integration. In the 19th and 20th centuries, immigration provided the required resources to fuel growth in many economies. Today the context is totally different. One of the main elements required for a company to have the capacity to receive and welcome immigrant employees is management's ability to lead a multicultural workforce. Using the work environment for integration is only successful if jobs are available and when the skills available match job requirements. Immigration and upskilling must be engineered together. The Swedish government's programme is an interesting example.

Although the government wants new immigrants to quickly find a workplace that is relevant to their existing individual education and experience, it's not always possible. Add to this disconnect, a shortage of labour in many industries and a golden opportunity arises. In 2015, this situation in the wood construction industry in Småland, Sweden, led to the design and implementation of a 35-week pilot in industrial construction. The overall objective of the project was to better match foreign job seekers' skills to the needs of the current labour market. Participants were migrants and refugees with permission to stay and work in Sweden. The pro-gramme allows small and medium-sized wood and furniture-mak-ing companies to hire people from other countries who have a mother-tongue other than Swedish. It is a tailor-made upskilling initiative for companies in the wooden housing construction indus-try: the 'buyers' are the future employers. This collaboration allows newly arrived immigrants to quickly establish themselves and build greater understanding of the labour market[117]. It facilitates adaptation to their new home and increases opportunities to work through learning new skills.

Today, this fast-track skills training ensures vacancies are filled through the provision of a highly skilled workforce. It is a collab-oration between DG Migration in Sweden; Vinnova, the Swedish Public Employment Service; and the Wood Centre, TRÄCEN-TRUM, the Industry Cluster collaboration organisation. TRÄCEN-TRUM provides the training, and its member companies provide locations for skills practice and on-the-job training. The project matches small - and medium - sized wood and furniture-producers in Småland, with participants enrolled in the programme, within the framework of the Wood Centre's Employment Service agreement.

The course consists of building bird houses, dog houses, and playhouses for children, and then a small 25 m² cottage. The training covers Swedish material theory (wood), building theory, workplace rules, Swedish workplace culture, values, hard and soft skills, role-play, and also has a personal coaching component. The 12-week programme entails on-the-job training at selected companies. Approximately 75% of participants obtain employment upon completion of the training. The project is an important contributor to secure industry recruitment *and* an important tool for integration and inclusion.

In 2018, the <u>Swedish Agency for Growth</u> granted 4,150,860 kr ($454,114) to the Wood Centre for their 'Easier Road to Work' project[118]. The funding supports further development of the successful pilot methodology. How scalable, or easily deployed to other industries and locations is this programme? How sustainable are these kinds of initiatives? Integration through upskilling is a paradigm shift for immigration and integration policies, but if successful, it would be embedded in a national skills strategy and provide, in part, a solution framework for the immigration crisis.

Main Messages

Jobs, and job vacancies, do not remain in the same location forever. Eventually, when faced with no other viable option, companies move jobs to where they can easily find a skilled, good-value workforce. Government leaders are in the driver's seats. They can catch this unique opportunity and keep pace with other growth-oriented countries… or miss it, through lack of vision and investments in their own workforce.

As main economic, education, and labour policy-makers; governments must invest massively and rapidly in their workforce. The estimated cost of upskilling – which includes hundreds of hours of training, salaries and other assistance – is over €10,000 per individual participant. This is a very powerful message to citizens who are worried about losing their jobs to automation, as well as to companies who are suffering from a lack of local skilled workforce.

Will public policies and training providers adapt fast enough to enable the huge shift needed to address upskilling requirements? Will organisations be able to use upskilling to fill vacant positions and ensure a positive flow of prepared employees? This is new behaviour for the majority of governments, workers and organisations. It repositions the workforce as the most dominant element of the market. Although this is radical thinking, there are signs that work, and workers, are already evolving. Whether governments and corporations change their thinking or not, the inception of a talent-driven job market has begun and will only accelerate, as the supplier-driven market recedes.

Chapter 9: Workforce Planning Priorities

The workforce planning movement has done much to advance the concept of strategic management of people and roles. The credo of workforce planning is simple. Get the right people, for the right job, with the right skills, at the right time, for the right price. It highlights the need for HR processes and procedures to be integrated into the broader landscape of business planning. It also gives weight to the argument that HR should be considered a strategic element for ensuring the ongoing success and effective operations of a business. Far from the required headcount that was once a 'one-line nod' to personnel management on the profit & loss statement, workforce planning has brought the need for strategic people management to the forefront. Taking a quick look at its history, benefits and short-comings for the digital age, we consider how workforce planning can be leveraged to build a truly collaborative and strategic approach to upskilling the workforce.

About Workforce Planning

A 2017 PwC survey of 20 CEOs, commissioned by the Luxembourg government, shows that workforce planning is still, to a large extent, in its infancy. The survey asked respondents if they had a digital transformation plan. About 90% answered that they had a plan in place, but a mere 10% of those plans had considered the implications and consequences of the digital transformation on the company's human resources. We see this topic rising to the top of HR executives' agendas everywhere. But planning, done correctly, is a demanding exercise. Many, if not most, HR executives are still struggling to address all the critical elements that provide systematic, lasting solutions.

A significant component of the solution is the planning timeframe that most organisations use. As humans, we have a widely varying capacity to plan and project into the future. Organisations, on the other hand, seem to uniformly adhere to a planning process that provides a one-year detailed outlook and a less detailed, three- to five-year forecast. The rationale behind this approach is relatively sound. The further out a company plans; the more variables must be considered. Of course, there are always elements that fall outside the control of the plan, no matter how well-designed. Even though there will always be unforeseen, and unforeseeable, variables, most will agree that it is much easier to plan for tomorrow than for next year.

Elements of Workforce Panning

The intent of many workforce planning exercises is to understand future competency requirements so that the company can achieve its objectives. HR, usually supported by consultants, spends a considerable amount of time setting up competency profiles for clusters of positions, and interpreting workforce evolution (size, type, experience, knowledge and skill). If we consider the complexity outlined previously, trying to make accurate predictions based on competency requirements up to five years in the future, would be tough for the best HR professionals.

One could predict, in general terms, generic competencies based on sectorial trends. For example, if you are in the automotive industry, you know electric or hydrogen cars will be the norm going forward, and that virtually everyone is working on autonomous cars. You also know that consumption modes are changing (e-commerce, virtual showroom), which means that business models are likely to change, for example, the ownership model and services associated with autonomous cars may be quite different. You can predict that in the next five to ten years, factories which produce petrol-driven engines will switch to electric engine manufacturing, and that robots on the production line will take over more and more activities.

This long-term view or forecast can indeed be quite useful. But first, the industry must determine what the future holds. Business must develop a clear vision of the potential futures for *individual* segments, and predict the speed of change, which is not really certain at all. To anticipate the potential for change on the horizon, we must review an array of elements:

Impacts of technology trends and developments; not just directly related to the company, but across industry segments. For example,

- new consumption modes: e-commerce, mobile banking, etc.

- new technology: gaming, project planning, communication, customer relationship management (CRM)

- digital transformation markers: social and process AI, chatbots, mobile and fixed robotics, advanced materials in manufacturing

Historical and statistical data such as company mobility patterns: internal moves, employee exits or hires, current employees' competencies, average attrition rate, known retirements, etc.

Operational forecasts such as opening, transformation and closure of business units, new positions needed (data scientists, coders, web designer, cyber security analysts, etc.), future competency requirements, and potential talent shortages

Change in the labour model, markets and geographies including the rise of freelancers and internationalisation of the workforce, job openings in new regions, and the link between market availability of talents and local or international business requirements

Regulatory and budget constraints such as new regulations or tariff adjustments between the US-China or EU-Japan, which severely influence commercial success

Although the combination of these elements seems very complex and daunting for the normal HR team, they are all linked. How organisations anticipate impacts and include these elements in their digital transformation plans, clearly influences HR policies, the organisation, and ultimately its performance.

Adaptation of Technology

One of the advantages of the explosion of HR technology today is that tools exist to assist this massive HR paradigm shift and to forecast, with relative accuracy, many of these critical elements. The claim to fame of current workforce planning technology is that it can manage worker profiles and ensure high-value candidate retention throughout the entire employee lifecycle. Whether the company is recruiting, deploying workers, or trying to optimise an individual's contribution, WFP technology keeps track of their goals, professional development, and pay rate. It can even assess key factors against the main competitors. To accomplish this feat, WFP technology uses scenario planning, predictive algorithms and a variety of other (mostly) cloud-based analytics to let managers know who is ready for a promotion, has the skills needed for a new job, and when it might be time to grant a raise for a job well-done or to ward off the competition.

The technology can even assess the effectiveness of employee benefits and steer HR away from measures that have a low-impact on employee retention or satisfaction. WFP technology allows organisations to compare unstructured data or even open text competency information to existing or future job requirements... in just a few seconds. It can look at future recruiting needs, potential costs and investments. It can even create better understanding of the social climate that influences employee well-being and company branding. The vast and relatively flexible capacity of many HR applications allows worldwide benchmarking, and assessment of the company's public image, to ensure it is attractive to potential workers.

Depending upon the scale of technology investment, it can 'crunch' data elements to predict the maturity of digitisation timelines one or two years in the future, forecast existing position requirements (eg type and number) and future gaps. This predictive technology is so powerful, that it can forecast, regardless of actual projections, the digital evolution following the 'normal pace' of investment in a specific industry. In essence, it gives organisations the ability to predict current and future jobs based on general market evolution.

Markets are moving fast. This versatility allows HR departments to work hand-in-hand with the C-Suite to consider a variety of factors from different angles. It allows the organisation to be agile in adapting their strategic planning and annual budgeting cycle to the speed and direction of the market. By focusing on the changes needed for workers to stay current with existing and future job opportunities, upskilling becomes a consistent and frequent activity. Shifting from annual workforce planning, to regular agile workforce skills planning exercises allows companies to skip complex competency mapping. Proceeding directly to the individual level, organisations quickly analyse which employees can perform which job, allowing them to keep pace with innovation and manage resource investments effectively. This innovative approach to people management, means that companies can embark, with their employees, on agile reskilling exercises.

Evolution of HR Models

The Ulrich HR model from the late 1990s, suggested splitting the strategic and operationally-focused activities. Segregating processes from 'business partner' functions enables HR to work more closely with the business and to create a more effective, happier and healthier organisation. By better understanding the business, HR more easily becomes a trusted advisor. The world has changed dramatically since the creation of the Ulrich model. Yet 20 years later, this function still struggles to attain these goals. One thing remains the same… the necessity for HR departments to be even closer to the business, Digital Officers, and the Executive Committee. Organisations must accurately forecast the market's acceptance of their offering, and the potential for a product, service or a combination of the two, to be successful. They need to understand factors that are impacting their ability to sell (including available resources and workers). Those informed and savvy organisations understand that their workforce is tied to their strategy, which is tied to their offering, which is tied to the marketplace. This, in turn is all tied to the evolution of opinions, knowledge and shifting consumer beliefs.

Corporations see the benefit of taking a longer perspective regarding personnel management and pushing the horizon as far as possible into the future. Today it is even more critical for HR to provide solutions that fit not only the business, but their employees' needs. They must understand the organisation and short- and medium-term trends in the marketplace. Having an agile mechanism that monitors existing jobs, the transformation required, and potential new/future positions, is key for success. Organisational change and learning systems are key factors for corporations to maintain high-quality client service and feed the market their products/services.

Change is here to stay. The competition for resources will only increase. All factors indicate that, although robots or other automation will usurp and reduce jobs in some areas, many more functions will spring up around this technology transformation, causing expanded needs in other areas. Technology influencing their products and/or services, is also impacting their ability to get their product to market, and in a large part, their people's ability to progress and/or evolve on the job. Workforce planning technology is a gateway to connecting strategy to people management. Done correctly, it can lead to better employee engagement and competency management.

Example: Robotics

Robotic Process Automation is being installed in the accounting departments of many organisations. We can surmise that we must reskill accountants to take on data or GDPR analyst work. Knowing that an automated warehouse is opening in nine months, we can teach workers to deal with Automatic Guided Vehicles or new warehouse interfaces, while reskilling others as coders for other departments.

Workforce Skills Planning Evolution and Benefits

This new way of thinking in terms of WFSP (Workforce Skills Planning) clearly supports change by institutionalising reskilling and mobility. As this becomes the norm, workers see employers' commitment for ongoing reskilling (employability). This shift supports employee engagement and company branding, which in turn, will create a better capacity to recruit talent even from shrinking resource pools.

The current pace of planning (mostly annually), and the general state and quality of analysis equipment, proves that a future is only 'certain' 9 to 15 months out. The steps associated with annual workforce planning exercises are relatively simple on the surface. Yet done correctly, the process must include virtually everyone in the organisation and even be agile enough to morph within the normal timeframe.

The stages begin to look much like a continuous strategic planning cycle. The yearly budget and forecasting cycles become just an indicator, as more information is gathered and used continuously to make decisions that impact future resourcing. The steps are simple...

1. **Gather** as much **information** as possible related to the composition of the workforce, for example the split between permanent and part-time workers, type of work, strategic information and operational plans. This includes back office, ICT, marketing and sales plans. A much-overlooked element in this step is any workflow or process analysis that shows where current bottlenecks are occurring and if they are related to lack of personnel. Statistics, such as employee turnover, promotions, discipline and source of potential workers to fill gaps are also important

2. **Analyse** the **information** in terms of the current personnel and short -to long-term development plans in each division/department. Map personnel requirements with strategic and business plans, and compare to existing personnel and roles

3. **Develop** and **implement** a plan to **fill gaps** – taking into consideration finances, reassignment of under-utilised personnel to high-need locations/jobs, training requirements, potential external sources for personnel, and communication with management about workforce projections

4. **Monitor** and **revise** the plan based upon successes and the changing needs of the organisation

If all these elements work well, the business and its strategy for managing and renewing its people, will be in lock-step. The organisation will indeed have the right people, with the right skills, to fill the right roles, at the right time, for the right price. Workforce planning can prevent loss and/or poaching of high-value individuals, and employee obsolescence caused by planned operational or technological change. What it won't prevent is the risk to the personnel if the organisation starts downsizing or right-scaling its workforce.

Accelerated change is not always due to technological innovation. For example, recently, Diesel Gate caused stock prices to plummet, the markets for these cars to disappear, and pushed consumers to migrate away from diesel quickly. This all happened at a speed that was not anticipated by most car manufacturer. The scandal caused changes in the way people all over the world view diesel engines, emissions testing and CO_2 reporting legislation. Even the software developed for the automotive industry is under review, with many saying that it is time for open-source coding that can be scrutinised by the general coding population. Stock prices fell, investment funds suffered, and people went to jail. The actions of this one company led to the deeper scrutiny of many. The legal ramification will continue to unfold for years to come.

There will always be a certain percentage of unknown ecological factors and constraints such as the acceleration of climate change, that will definitely have an unanticipated impact. The question then becomes how to reduce these 'unknowns' and ensure the organisation has a well-thought-through path to follow, once markers or indicators are spotted. WFP tools have allowed managers to become more tuned to employee contribution, recognition, retention and market forces that influence these factors.

Management has a huge advantage when it engages completely in the success of the company and its workforce. The problem today is that most companies view the important element of strategic planning as management's job only. What is missing for many is the organisational mind-set and targeted conversations that allows the whole company to become focused on the future.

A mindset that encourages every worker to look for signs that their future is changing.

Changing the Organisation's Mindset

Workforce planning focuses on finding the right mix between the type, price and number of workers, for current and projected roles. Although it does consider workers' skills and knowledge as assets, it does not fully consider employee motivation, intellectual or relationship capital.

Most WFP technology has some sort of scenario planning embedded in it, which allows an organisation to begin to think about alternate futures. The Introduction of Scenario Thinking in WFP has advantages. Energising and exciting people about the future, it creates an agile organisation that is ready to turn when markers emerge on the horizon. It allows the company to identify markers or indicators that guide decision-making. Potential futures have identifiable circumstances that, as they change, point in one direction or another. Upskilling initiatives that use scenario planning, disseminate scenario thinking through the whole organisation. For upskilling initiatives, scenario planning uses steps to engage the population, choose and expand upon likely scenarios, and to develop a set of early indicators that will guide and align the whole organisation.

More than just a static planning exercise, scenario planning teaches everyone in the organisation to keep an eye on the future to become observers; watching for indicators to appear. This process creates a more agile and curious mind-set within the organisation. It encourages all stakeholders to challenge the status quo and to engage in open discussion about possibilities and probabilities. The ongoing conversation sparked by WFP scenario planning can align virtually everyone in the organisation. Developing and watching for targets, empowers everyone to challenge commonly held assumptions through meaningful and deep conversation that helps predict the future.

Ideal Planning Horizon

Obviously, it's difficult to fully predict the future two to five years down the road, but a 9- to 18-month outlook is pretty clear for most managers. Decisions to sign purchase orders are taken regularly, and projects are confidently deployed with a rather reliable go-live date. Even individuals, can accurately work with a 9- to 18-month horizon. Any change is far enough in the future to give time to adapt and embrace the new reality. It provides enough of a burning platform to motivate, yet allows time for employees to acquire skills that will address competency issues for a new job on the horizon. It is also the correct term for both companies and individuals to be more or less 90% certain that something will really occur. This means that individuals can invest the time and effort in acquiring new skills, with a clear and secure job in perspective. HR also has time to engage in discussions with individuals, prepare communication and training plans and organise new skills training. Technology is the catalyst for this new paradigm. It enables workforce planning and provides new capability. Indeed, many of the exercises today, use this enabling technology to skip rapidly through major analysis, easily matching potential jobs with individual competencies and identifying the skills gap in a few days.

Fatal Shortcomings for WFP

The intent of WFP is to maintain happy and productive workers, but potentially fatal short-comings in approaches are clearly worth addressing. Although workforce planning usually takes place in conjunction with strategic planning, even today, HR is frequently not at the table. Instead of being an integral component, or pillar of the strategic planning process, most organisations still use personnel projections as an add-on to strategy. Management asks how workers can support their projected future, and not the more seminal question… How is our strategy being influenced by *all* the forces that impact the organisation? The following is a simpli-fied representation of what happens in most corporations but will suffice for this example.

Human resource cycles are usually based on a one-year outlook. Objectives are set and reviewed by management, and perfor-mance is tracked in this timeframe. Between this cycle of planning and evaluation, employees attend some training and sometimes have a conversation about their career with someone. HR's 'add-ed value' in this exercise is not always obvious. The cycle might incorporate some investment in training, systems, recruitment campaigns but, for the most part, the thought process in most companies is not focused on the people-side of the equation. Beyond the yearly cycle, most companies use grading systems based on pay-scale or promotions. A long-term development/ training plan is still a bit rare these days. High-potential candidate pools and tailored professional development plan are reserved for a very few. Workers must have faith that the planning cycle will consider their needs and aspirations. Still, companies know they cannot promise what they will not be able to deliver, so much information is left in limbo.

Main Messages

There are two problems with WFP being a management exercise instead of a collaboration between employees and other stake-holders. Today, we know that the more brains the better. A diverse set of inputs will get a better output.

Companies hate incertitude and the unknown. Most activities are based on plans, investments, and budget. Management wants to plan well in advance. This worked relatively well until recently when economic and technological cycles accelerated. In the past, the time between innovation and system changes was long enough to plan for amortisation and to schedule worker replacements in advance. Today innovation and technology advances have drastically shifted the time available to address change, disruptive solutions, accelerated product development and new competitors.

Individuals need to believe in the approach. Virtually every study on the future of work indicates that stakeholder engagement is critical to success, but much of what passes for planning and forecasting, takes place behind closed doors - or doors that are only opened a smidgen!

People read and listen to the news, they have friends and families working in different environments, even if they don't want to face reality, they know things happen and that the world is changing and accelerating. This does not mean they accept or embrace it.

We must refocus on the short- and medium-term. Companies and individuals must become more comfortable with a fluid and flexible approach that can pivot; customising the 'roadmap' to the future as indicators emerge. Companies understand the complexity of long-term planning but are not willing to dedicate the time and effort to engage employees to create a positive future outcome.

For upskilling to work, governments, corporations, unions, associations and individuals must all work together. For some, this means passing some control to those who need it. For others, it will be taking charge of activities that once were managed by others. The pattern and approach are clear. Accountability and collaboration are, and will always be, the mainstays of a successful, sustainable and productive upskilling initiative. Workforce Skills Planning must now be continuous and targeted on element of the WFSP cycle; reducing cost for governments and corporations, and stress for workers.

Chapter 10: Government Priorities

Governments play a critical dual role in upskilling initiatives. Ministers must consider how to provide a strong foundation of support for the development and implementation of upskilling initiatives for the general business population. They must also look internally at their own staff requirements for upskilling. From top civil servants to front-line workers charged with executing the day-to-day activities that keep governments moving, the time is now.

Environmental and health issues, Brexit, migration, cybersecurity, trade wars. Over the last three years, the news has provided many new problem statements for governments. The largest and most pressing is how to rapidly build world-class competencies. This chapter endeavours to answer some of the questions associated with these dilemmas.

Minister of Skills

In the last two years, the agenda for the EU Council of Ministers of Labour (EPSCO) has begun to include discussions regarding the digitalisation of work and the risks of automation to the workforce. We are running very late. With few exceptions, such as Germany, Luxembourg and Scandinavian countries, most of Ministers of Labour are stuck acting more like 'Ministers of Unemployment'. Pressed by public opinion, most countries have developed a curative approach to unemployment. They have not treated the real root cause; the need to match the unemployed to vacant positions using sensible upskilling initiatives.

When we look at growth in virtually every EU country, it is extremely difficult to identify any powerful and well-articulated national skills strategy. Integral to the healthy future of the EU and individual countries is a strategy that:

1) identifies and meaningfully forecasts the economic demand of the region, and

2) explains the local sourcing system

Apprenticeship, vocational training, immigration and collaboration with other countries are all solution elements. As a best practice solution, the German Minister of Labour recently published a report, Competency Needs by 2030, that forecasts the vertical, digital and soft skills competencies required by companies today, and in the near future. Some regions, such as Baden-Württemberg, Germany, have a long-standing tradition of expanding upon this type of strategy for their industries[119].

They take a collaborative approach and build relevant facilities, such as 'Learning Factories'. These support the strategy and plan with concrete and physical representation of their commitment to developing their population's skills. Without this clearly articulated, published and promoted strategy, each country is left to their own devices, deprived of the insight and strategy that creates the tight-fitting mosaic we require.

Governments are grappling to address skills governance and leadership. This challenge is reinforced by the complexity of many administrations and their focus on short-term, high-visibility solutions. Many governments, hand-cuffed by opposition, or slow archaic processes, are fighting just to create basic awareness around the need to upskill and prepare for the future in the general population. Add to this the need to design government roles that can rapidly address these critical issues, and we can see the challenge clearly.

Most people can name their Minister of Education, their Minister of Labour, and/or their Minister of the Economy ... but few people have even heard of a Minister of Skills. This comes as no surprise since the position doesn't even exist in most governments. If the Minister of Skills doesn't exist, though, who is responsible for ensuring a strategy that will enable workers to skill up in anticipation of the long-term needs of business and the market?

The Minister of Education, to some extent, is responsible for knowledge creation, development and apprenticeships. The Minister of Labour is also partly responsible for vocational training. The Minister of Economy controls the country's investment strategy, thereby impacting jobs. Of all the Ministries today, the Ministry of the Economy truly requires business support to ensure a vibrant and healthy economy. In reality, it has limited influence and power in terms of effective skills development programmes without the support of business.

A few governments understand the importance of installing a Minister of Skills. Ireland, the UK and India are examples of this innovative structural evolution.

Example: India

In India, the Minister of Skills Development is responsible for ...

- coordinating all skills development efforts across the country

- removing the disconnect between skilled manpower supply and demand

- building vocational and technical training frameworks

- upgrading and building new skills, and

- innovating current thinking – not only for existing jobs – but also for jobs that are yet to be created!

Upskilling the Civil Service

Upskilling civil servants should be a top priority for government. It may even be more important and urgent than undertaking an upskilling initiative in the private sector. While business is mainly focused on growth and profitability, governments must face a new type of crisis; developing a new set of required skills ... throughout bureaucracy.

Upskilling Civil Servant

There are many justifications for an upskilling policy that includes the entire administration. The overall need for digital effectiveness is one. The fact that we are so far behind on digitalisation in practically every segment of society, justifies a complete upskilling programme that reaches from leaders to front-line civil servants.

According to our analysis, the State, like other employers, will face just as much difficulty to attract talented people. Even in countries like Singapore, high remuneration for civil servants may not be sufficient. The new generation desires rapid career progression, opportunities to acquire skills and knowledge at an accelerated pace, and a dynamic workplace that recognises talent and accomplishment. Energising, motivating and upskilling the current public workforce will help the State meet its obligations and even provide higher service effectiveness, leading to greater customer satisfaction.

Upskilling civil servants from various ministries and administrations requires a tailored approach. The rationale is clear; the variety of initial education, lack of vocational training, rapid automation of administrative tasks, changes to key roles/tasks, such as designing and executing new policies, and even the government's interaction with the general public, require a considered approach. In a rapidly changing economy, governments and administrations must escape from 'catch-up' mode. They must understand societal changes and design innovative transformational policies that will keep the country, and its population, in step with digitalisation in all domains. This is very demanding for leaders, managers and staff who, we are sure, already feel increased 'digital weight' on their shoulders .

Any upskilling initiative must be fully integrated with e-government investments and policies. Most public services are already, to a certain extent, digitalised with forms and a variety of online pro-cessing, freeing bureaucrats and civil servants from rote tasks. An excellent example of this is the digitalisation of personal and corporate tax declarations. Thousands of civil servants in the Min-istries of Finance across the globe have been released from the rote task of transferring data from forms. This principle applies to any activity where completing and validating information is import-ant. For the Ministry of Health, Transport, or Agriculture... the key tasks now are supervision and control.

What happens to the people responsible for those rote tasks? Current possibilities include job cuts, transformation or relocating staff to different departments. Some limited upskilling initiatives and policies exist, but none that match the scale or robustness needed to upskill civil servants to ensure better, more effective use of public resources.

Assessing Value

Of course, with any large government initiative, at least part of the conversation revolves around value for money (or budget). Better use of public resources or taxpayers' funds are easy arguments but are only two ways to define benefit. Assessing the ROI of State upskilling is highly complex. Each administration would be required to compare its investment in upskilling to the probability or risk of failure in terms of the administration's mission and goals.

In most cases, the State's effectiveness would increase in some proportion to the higher competency of its staff, but tying productivity gains to skills acquisition, especially in the public service domain, could be daunting. Let's consider three different examples.

Example #1: Cybersecurity

Scenario #1: The Ministry of the Interior trained and upskilled a number of key specialists on the latest cybersecurity attack scenarios. Three months later, one specialist detected and prevented a new attack on potential at-risk targets. The agent prevented a major business continuity interruption and averted financial risk, without consequence to the company or the State. If the training did not take place, if the attack on the company's bank account succeeded; it would cause direct financial loss. The training investment contributed to business continuity success.

Scenario #2: The other option is that the State does not invest in training key specialists and the company suffers financial damage. Although the State suffers no direct consequence, the indirect aftermath of the successful attack could be far-reaching. Lack of confidence in security measures might cause companies to relocate to other regions or countries. Successful attacks could cause one or more companies to go bankrupt, etc. These outcomes, while not directly visible, will eventually have an impact on GDP and economic growth.

Example #2: Data Processing

The introduction of new data processing and analysis software allows tax declarations to be automatically completed, checked and explanations provided to tax controllers. This allows the tax controller to manage up to five times more tax declarations than previously possible. In a department of 100 people, reviewing 1000 declarations daily, about 70 jobs would disappear.

A proactive and anticipatory plan is certainly required. First, tax controllers using the new software must undergo intense training. This optimises resources and maximises use of the new system. Therefore, the State will see an immediate pay-off via payroll savings. Upskilling the remaining 70 workers pays off if new, productive functions are created or vacant positions can be filled via the correct, upgraded skills.

Example #3: Low Tech Limits

Low-skilled civil servants combined with low technology financing, limit business activities and the growth of investments. The administration becomes a bottleneck and, rather than being a growth multiplier, it becomes a barrier through lack of skills and technology. This is seen in offices that provide accreditation, authorisations or subsidies. The calculation of ROI includes upskilling costs, technology investments, and also loss associated with lack of management process improvements.

Almost anyone in the general population can clearly identify the cost of inaction or indecision that leaves low-quality, unproductive systems in place far too long. For the State, the ROI calculation for upskilling must also include savings from higher productivity and effectiveness that is triggered by technology and management process investment.

The Civil Servants' Perspective

Most governments and administrative leaders recognise the strategic importance of upskilling civil servants but do not have a concrete plan. Leaders have the impression that civil servants are not interested in changing or upgrading their skills portfolio. Many think that because civil servants hold the same job for years, they are not keen to change. This may be true for those who work in large administrations, organised as silos, with few external recruits and limited management changes. Generally, people believe that civil servants are mainly concerned with their jobs, the infrastructure that enables them to deliver properly, their career path and their financial packages. In other words, upskilling may not be at the top of their agenda. Yet, in periods of crisis such as health pandemics that require millions of people to be vaccinated, civil servants demonstrate their commitment to learning and their capacity to integrate new skills rapidly. Upskilling may only be seen as a patch to manage a crisis or a technical issue. Their upskilling solutions were never designed using a global framework, that defines job outcomes, new skill portfolios or professional development plans.

This side of the conversation has a variety of facets and perspectives. It ranges from Ministers' Cabinet Heads who are very agile, on top of new technology and designing forward looking policies, to civil servants working in understaffed regional offices with outdated equipment and limited interaction with the 'new economy'. It requires a substantial paradigm shift to the public sector's perspective on career management. One element influencing this shift currently is, unfortunately, the frequent natural and man-made disasters occurring around the world. The emergence of many radical and very complex international crises requires new knowledge and skills in central and local administrations. This indeed, may be the catalyst that drives the public service toward life-long learning and a continuous skills portfolio development model. Let's look at examples that illustrate these new challenges.

Example #1: Severe Situations

Civil and public servants are being asked to become experts in regularly occurring situations that are not only new, but of almost unimaginable severity. For example, populations across the globe are subject to increasingly hazardous weather conditions. Civil and public servants must manage, mitigate and prevent energy and weather risks and/or disasters, problem-solve to protect populations, and communicate effectively regarding many other dangerous situations. Very few of these skills are acquired during their initial job training. Yet the magnitude of knowledge and skill required to remediate large-scale emergencies requires gargantuan efforts, collaborated across many sectors.

The notorious earthquake disaster at Fukushima and subsequent tsunami, just weeks before its decommissioning, provides a snapshot of the extreme challenges many ministry staff now face.

Example #2: Policy Consequences

The second example is the consequences of policy. Decision such as Brexit have a huge impact on UK trade policy. Confronted with an unexpected referendum outcome, the UK, which, until recently, depended upon the EU Commission for trade expertise, is urgently rebuilding a complete skills portfolio on trade negotiation and agreements. This is an immensely technical area, covering the entire economy and intersecting with more than 200 countries. It requires civil servants with excellent negotiation skills, detailed and cutting-edge knowledge of the different economic sectors. The UK government has used external global recruitment and offered internal administration mobility to meet this challenge[120].

Example #3: Technology & Innovation for Public Safety

Increasingly, technological security threats are aimed at blocking State or administration functions. Some years ago, Estonia was almost paralysed by cyberattacks that created an incomparable threat to the economy and the State's sustainability. As well as mobilising quickly to solve the attacks, Estonia created an innovative intervention team and reworked policy to prevent future occurences. Each Estonian civil servant became a security ambassador to promote, teach and implement security for all, anytime, anywhere. The outcome included a cyber-defence unit, whose volunteers practice mitigation measures in case of another major online attack[121].

Approach for Government Leaders

Our experience at the EU and national levels, convinces us to propose a threefold approach:

1) tailored onboarding of leaders to ensure they act as role models

2) the introduction of innovation labs in public offices, and

3) a new framework for civil servant career management

1. Leaders First

Government ministers must lead by example. They must be the first to upskill themselves in strategic areas affected by new technology. They must take a concentrated and urgent approach to their personal upskilling initiatives. Wherever their work is, they must 1) have a solid technical background, 2) a clear understanding of their knowledge gaps, and 3) a plan to close them.

Understanding gaps is fundamental to success. In 2016, PwC, under a mandate from the EU Commission (DG GROW), organised a 2-hour boot camp for 28 EU Ministers of Economy and their advisors at the informal Competitiveness Summit[122]. The boot camp was organised around six different growing technologies: robotics, cybersecurity, 3D printing, drones, coding and connected cars. Fast-track demonstrations provided by entrepreneurs, were designed to help the ministers understand the technology, current barriers to development and adoption, and market opportunities. For most of them, it was their first real experience manipulating their own drone[122].

Without fast-track upskilling and practical experience on new emerging technologies, ministers are at high risk of forming the wrong vision and/or strategy.

In President Hollande's government, the Minister of Economy, who held the position for more than two years, resigned to take a university economic affairs programme. This is a great example of motivated intention to upskill for the future, but as the Minister of Economy, it would be more credible and have more impact if he had upskilled before his appointment or even during his mandate.

Ministers and administration heads, as well as company CEOs, are role models and must set the example for upskilling. By undertaking a programme personally, they officially demonstrate that all leaders must focus on learning to be efficient and successful in their role. This sends a strong message that change starts with top management.

2. Innovation Labs

Visits with the Minister of Finance in the UAE (Dubai), take place in the ministry's innovation lab. This facility supports co-design, co-innovation, exchange of best practices, and presents live demonstrations of new technology. It is a sandbox for civil servants to discover, understand and visualise the key trends affecting their work. By organising boot camps and hackathons that include the private sector, they imagine what the work of the future will be. This is a great example of best-practice that many ministries and administrations can adopt.

Each ministry (Finance, Economy, Labour and Education) should have its own innovation and co-design space where the administration can play with the future. Meeting places where people can come together to build a common vision, are a very efficient tool. They provide a place where leaders, managers and staff, can focus and visualise the pros and cons of new technology and imagine the future using specific objectives.

3. A New Framework

We propose a new career management and upskilling framework for civil servants. A framework that assists civil servants in creating new solutions for managing the highly complex problems of today, yet builds appropriate objectives that motivate and support sustainable career development for the future.

The objective of this new career framework is to provide the State with the most effective and motivated agents. Civil servants ensure the education, prosperity, sustainability, employability and security of all citizens. If they are to achieve this mission, they must already have a solid initial education and appropriate degrees. For those who have been in the same function, perhaps for years, as well as for new recruits, investment in continuous learning throughout their whole career is required. This may seem like an insurmountable task, but broken down into the five framework dimensions they become easily executable:

1. **Make internal mobility a priority:** This is a first step toward augmenting learning options throughout a civil servant's career. Valuing accelerated career paths, financial rewards, or the intellectual and network capital gained in a succession of roles and/or functions, will allow a department or ministry to bring conversations about career management and mobility into the mainstream. This is not about punishing those who cannot change. It's about supporting those who accept standardised skills development processes from the outset. On-boarding, orientation to life-long learning, and technical support are critical success elements.

2. **Measure and Manage Skills Portfolios:** Public affairs skills

portfolio management requires the creation of new, or the transformation of thousands of existing, responsibilities. Organising the best match and demonstrating the variety of opportunities for civil servants, is enabled by assessing their current skills portfolio, motivation level and personal drivers. Today, public competitions are used to fill new jobs in most public administrations. The selection of civil servants is limited to people looking for a new career and who are already aware of their own skills. Most civil servants have little, if any, idea of jobs they could apply for or where the best job opportunities can be found. They under-assess their own skills portfolio and concurrently, are not even aware of the evolving skills required for their current job. Although this lack of awareness might be a source of concern, ultimately, it is a fantastic opportunity for the State to leverage an existing resource pool of motivated civil servants.

3. **Towards an ambitious workforce planning exercise:** Matching personal skills and assessing motivation to acquire new job skills affords HR leaders a unique opportunity. Using forward-looking workforce planning tools, they can design scenarios that encompass various functions, and evaluate the financial impact of technology introductions on the daily work of civil servants. For example, one scenario could look at the impact of automation on day-to-day activities in certain areas, including potential attrition due to retirement, job changes, new missions, historical turnover and other factors.

The Dutch police have launched a full workforce planning process aimed at understanding jobs, skills and the number of workers projected to be needed over next five years[123]. This co-designed and engaged implementation includes key direct stakeholders and ensures the outcome is sustainable and relevant to all.

4. **Link upskilling and mobility to increasing remuneration:** Salary increases can be a major driver for most civil servants. This financial reward could be used to motivate staff to invest their time and energy in acquiring new skills for a specific professional opportunity. Special incentives for intense training linked to a new qualification, can be a strong cultural shift accelerator and for the State to see a return on investment. For private sector providers, a performance fee model can incentivise success and pedagogical innovations.

The national civil servant framework for upskilling is critical to enable higher motivation, culture change, and accelerated acquisition of skills. It creates a better match between new and/or transformed jobs and ambitious civil servants. Closing the skills gap with revamped vocational training policies, curricula and training providers enables effective workforce planning. New job requirements, matched to civil servants' skills portfolio (assessments), give the State a clear view of the consolidated skills gap in their entire administration.

Revamping the vocational training policy to address the skills gap is a top priority which saves money and resources. Focused and purposeful vocational training is key. More targeted training with higher investment per person, produces greater impact than small, generic, old-fashioned training offered to everyone. This primary objective of workforce planning can be a key input for the new specifications of public tenders, selecting curricula and training providers.

5. **Create a tailored skills strategy for ministries and administrations:** A tailored upskilling strategy by ministry and administration can complement a national framework perfectly. From a bottom-up perspective, it is important to show workers a set

of opportunities in different departments or administrations at their level. Civil servants should experience the change positively and understand that their future is linked to upskilling.

Each ministry and/or administration defines skill priorities that support the implementation of their political priorities. This strategy, which consolidates and creates a snapshot of these skills, enables sourcing and recruiting solutions. This exercise must fully complements the technology investment strategy. This is a complex, but highly valuable exercise that ensures the success of on-the-ground public policy implementation. In fact, each new ministry policy should include a skills gap assessment, which analyses civil servants in that region and determines if they are equipped with the correct skills to implement the new policy successfully. Upskilling should become mainstream and increasingly tied to overall interest and job satisfaction.

Through our work with international governments, accelerating the economy's digital transformation, we have seen smart national policies, with relevant objectives and adequate resources, blocked during regional implementations. The main issue is lack of understanding, lack of the correct skill sets and the unfortunate actions of regional civil servants stuck in outdated business models of the former 'tangible-asset' economies.

Primary Targets

Our analysis of key administrations that employ the highest number of civil servants, indicates that there are good, and very strategic reason for the State to proceed with upskilling. They include security, competitiveness, tax revenue, and education. Each domain has as a multiplier effect on the private sector. For example, if security is ensured, tourism and foreign investments flourish.

The main question in this area is ... Which is better? A State that leads its population toward a bright future or one that is always playing catch-up?

Primary targets for initial upskilling projects are military, education, energy, industry, trade, and critical infrastructure. Related and required skills can be determined and prioritised among the different ministries and administrations. Access to important assessment criteria allows stakeholders to determine priorities related to the customary burning platforms. Existing skills portfolio, level of qualification, average age, etc., can be gaged against the risk of automation, impact on society or competitiveness, and level of strategic activity. This criteria list provides not only a starter set but demonstrates the complexity and importance of the problem.

Different criteria will not carry the same weight for each administration. Central administration, for example, is close to political power hubs, and benefits from prime information, access to excellent specialists and training. While regional administrations, without access to the knowledge enjoyed elsewhere, struggle to catch up with new policies and trends.

Primary targets for initial upskilling projects					
	Education	Military	Tax	Police	Healthcare
Strategic activity	YES	YES	YES	YES	YES
Impact on society	HIGH	LOW	LOW	HIGH	HIGH
Average age	MEDIUM	MEDIUM	HIGH	LOW	HIGH
Impact on competitiveness	HIGH	LOW	LOW	HIGH	MEDIUM
Level of initial qualification	AVERAGE	AVERAGE	MEDIUM	LOW	MEDIUM
Risk of automation	NONE	MEDIUM	HIGH	LOW	MEDIUM

Table #14: Primary Targets for Initial Upskilling Projects

The military is the only administration currently managing staff skills portfolios and actively using a very detailed process to close the skills gap. Over the last 70 years, the army has integrated many innovations and technology, consequently upgrading the skills portfolio of the troops. This evolutionary process is in their DNA. Their experience in upskilling is very valuable and should be leveraged by other administrations and private sectors. It is practical, condensed, precise and recognised by peers as a high-quality process.

The Ministry of Finance, with large numbers of civil servants in tax administration, for example, is impacted by automating technology. It must provide new career paths for its staff. Upskilling is clearly a solution that can leverage knowledge of state processes for new functions in other departments.

The Minister of Interior has a more complex situation to manage with police staff. The increasing pressure for police officers to perform to strict standards, makes their job highly sensitive and more subject to external pressure. Even if they upskill and update initial training content, their best platform is on-the-ground learning that builds experience from a realistic perspective.

The healthcare system presents different challenges: scarcity of general practitioners, the ageing working population, technology advances in a plethora of medical fields and intense pressure on healthcare professionals, all coalesce to form more and more stress as they progress through their career. Once again, training on new technology and new protocols require a forward-looking competency plan.

Main Messages

Will upskilling lead to a more effective public service? Of course. Although it is clear that the civil servants' success factors should be different from business, they must be upskilled; not only in public service or vocational training, but in shared curricula with private employees. Administration must develop a global framework for the entire government, that allows a more tailored approach by ministry or segment. Governments can learn from the military, which has an effective on-going upskilling programme. Priority professions to upskill among civil servants are teachers, policy developer, and front-line officers. Although the ROI and off-setting behavioural implications might be more difficult to quantify, they are substantial.

Defining new, realistic job requirements for all civil servants could relieve much stress. In France, in 1989 and 2009 the government implemented workforce planning exercises for all areas of its administration. Unfortunately, this initiative did not translate into many concrete actions. The complexity of tackling a problem of that size, the absence of ongoing planning models and the myopic views of managers are just a few of the hinderances. We must heed the lessons from this failure and learn from them. The challenges raised by the acceleration of the global tech economy and the succession of complex crises demand action.

Given the State's strategic importance in this fast-paced changing environment, it is a top priority to increase awareness and upskill administrations, leaders and managers. Initial training, age, time to pension, digital agility, personal environment and exposure to the private and international economy are some of the factors that will influence the acceptance of upskilling programmes. Yet, understanding technology and new systems, allows administrations to design forward-looking policies. Investing in technology and new processes that reduce the need for resources that perform basic, repetitive tasks, frees up civil servants to focus on high value activities. Technology can assist in the execution of activity, identification within career paths and creating remuneration packages. A tailored upskilling process, with professional and financial rewards for the most engaged and talented civil servants, is absolutely required to ensure security, sustainability, prosperity and excellence.

For the general population, although we cannot forecast what jobs the future holds, we know that the most in-demand functions today did not exist ten years ago. We do know, however, that companies and individuals must prepare for future jobs, in a radically different way than today. High-quality, tailored training, appropriate incentives and voluntarily participation are the foundation for successfully moving workers to new functions. The government plays an integral role in creating and maintaining this landscape and ensuring that there are highly-skilled workers for future job.

Chapter 11. Educational Priorities

With the exponential growth of societal knowledge, more than any other civil servants, teachers' roles are becoming increasingly complex. Yet they receive very limited continuous training. This disconnects them from the real economic world and from their students.

Few individuals have the foresight to upskill themselves, or the good fortune to live in countries where upskilling is encouraged and supported robustly by productive government strategies. We have a perfect storm of unskilled workers and unfillable jobs. It is causing a raging talent war that forces organisations to compete for the few who are appropriately skilled for the digital age. In the last chapter we discussed the government's role in creating a rich and exciting environment for future workers. This chapter deals specifically with the educational system responsible for equipping students with knowledge and skills for a changing world.

To some extent, the Ministry of Education may be the least prepared for the digital revolution and, based solely on its influence, this ministry is probably the government body most in need of upskilling. This ministry has an enormous influence on society. Upskilling it and the associated teachers and professors, is strategic but complex.

Education: Critical Contribution to Success

Teachers from primary school to university, were once the only source of knowledge. Schools and universities used indisputable teachers and well-recognised thought-leaders to present knowledge. Today, students have access to multiple sources of knowledge and do not hesitate to challenge the professors' statements or pedagogy. This is a new phenomenon that requires a large and very intense upskilling for teachers. Yet most schools continue to focus on ancient knowledge assets and learning devices such as outdated books and lessons. Teachers continued to teach the way they were taught to teach, decades ago. Educational systems, from primary school to university, have remained fixed in a very traditional model, making limited modifications to programmes and avoiding conflicts with teachers and unions by focusing on the status quo.

Some educational policy leaders have, however, made changes aimed at enabling students to take full advantage of the technological revolution. Unfortunately, measures are more about providing iPads and other tech-enabled equipment, rather than teaching new knowledge such as programming skills. But at least this is a start.

Moving Inefficiency to Practical Benefit

In his book, World Class, How to Build a 21st Century School System, Andreas Schleicher, OECD Director for Education and Skills (OECD Programme) and coordinator of the Programme for International Student Assessment (PISA), detailed rationale and recommendations for a significant reshaping of the school system. His starting point was a shocking statistic. In 2015, for the 70 high- and middle-income countries participating in the PISA test, almost 50% of students did not posess basic reading and mathematics skills. Especially shocking, when educational expenditure rose by almost by 20% during the last decade. He also confirmed, using many examples of educational excellence, that learning outcomes can be significantly increased even for the most disadvantaged populations. Clearly, a change must be made.

The signals are there. High numbers of people without basic reading and mathematics skills, increasing NEET and the growing mismatch between the workforce supply and skills demand, all point to major challenges. The education system, designed after the second world war, must adapt to better meet society's future needs.

Most educational curricula do not include, or encourage, teaching methods that focus on new cognitive or leadership skills. Even though they are acknowledged to be the most likely baseline skills for all future jobs. Many faculties don't provide a current perspective on jobs or the job market. This allows thousands of students to follow psychology or geography programmes, for example, without knowing how many jobs are, or will be, available and potential qualification requirements.

High NEET percentages clearly signal the increasing disconnection between the education system, business and society. They portent the loss of credibility, as students and parents begin to doubt the efficacy of both teachers and teaching methods. We see that the trust society has placed in teachers, and the system, is eroding quickly. Constituents are questioning teachers':

1) ability to provide the right knowledge: a transversal set of information, applicable to many different types of jobs, and

2) teaching style: that must encourage students to think critically and creatively for themselves. Indeed, to think outside of the box, and apply learning to a variety of situations and challenges, may be the most important skill one can learn at any age.

To regain students' and parents' confidence, we must get back to the basic levels of education. We must dare to change. The system must safeguard students' fundamental right to basic skills such as reading and mathematics. Beyond this, educational systems must ensure that students are prepared for future jobs and the job market. The central objective must increasingly become the students' appetite for learning across many topics. The ability to acquire information from different fields, multi-disciplined thinking and transforming knowledge to skill, is key to future jobs. We must all work together to help ensure students can choose studies that prepare them to be productive, functioning members of the workforce and society. In this major educational paradigm shift, life-long learning and rapid knowledge acquisition is fundamental.

What to learn then becomes a new responsibility. Learning to learn is certainly a skill that is not taught in many schools today but will become one of the most strategic in the whole educational framework. For students, the system must provide guidance and support for selecting their areas of study, not just according to their personal interests and aspirations, but also according to what society needs. Students and adult professionals alike, have a responsibility to know what they need to learn and a duty to manage their knowledge. They must understand what is missing in terms of potential job capabilities and know how to fill the gaps.

The depreciation of our acquired knowledge and skills is accelerating. In a world characterised by the daily creation of a massive collective quantity of new knowledge, we must be cognisant of our learning responsibilities. Designing, organising, and supporting upskilling strategies is imperative. New educational objectives must be set. Strategies must be buttressed by business' and governments' commitment to life-long learning (upskilling); permitting the rapid and frequent acquisition of valuable skills and knowledge.

If a worker stops acquiring new knowledge and skills for more than six months, their portfolio will begin to depreciate rapidly. This is what happens to the unemployed who are disconnected from their professional environment for some months.

Finland's profound educational reform (described in Chapter #7: Financing Solutions) is a strong testament to the opportunity and positive results that flow from redefining current systems and pedagogy. Educational systems must use clear knowledge and skills acquisition objectives, that are aligned to societal and economic demands. Although it seems daunting, this is far less challenging than the economic devastation that an unemployable population will produce.

Vocational Training System

About 40 million young people in OECD countries are not in education, employment or training, so-called NEET (see Chapter #2: Challenge for Government). This is the equivalent of 15% of youth aged 15 to 29. Two-thirds of them are not even looking for work. This clearly demonstrates the current education system's inefficiency in transmitting the level of knowledge and skills that students need to be able to participate fully in the economy. The latest OECD research indicates that young employees are subject to a higher risk of job automation[124]. Potentially, this could result in even higher youth unemployment. As mentioned in Chapter #1, according to OECD analysis, low-skilled adults have the highest risk of losing their job to automation[9]. They are more than three times *less* likely to have participated in on-the-job training over a 12-month period, than workers in non-automatable positions. On average, this high-risk group receives 29 hours less job-related training annually than high-skilled workers.

Adult learning programmes are fantastic instruments to upskill people. Vocational training, that includes learning on the job, is certainly a primary avenue to acquire new knowledge and skills for a large percentage of the working population. It targets the right people and focuses on specific learning and quality objective; providing participants with new measurable skills. Industry associations historically provided well-organised, high-quality, external vocational training curricula, instructors and classes. However, the digital revolution and the rapid evolution of new machines, means that most curricula and training equipment have become obsolete. The frequency of hardware upgrades has also driven new equipment costs through the roof. In general, industry associations no longer have the financial wherewithal and human resources to rapidly build new training programmes. Consequently, large firms are reinventing the curriculum for the development of their people, while SMEs are facing major difficulties to find relevant and cost-effective training solutions.

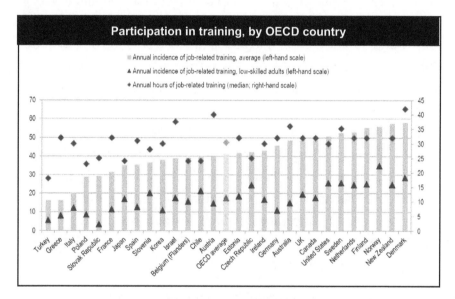

Figure #15: Training of Low-skilled Adults

A New Path Forward

A new approach to learning must be conceived. Ensuring that the right skills are coming available as the economy requires them, is a huge mandate for governments. If the vocational training system fails to address the critical and present demand for skills in this shifting business and economic landscape, our next generation will have little chance of success. It is time for governments to align all ministries to focus on supporting the future success of its workers. The path is long and fraught with risks, but Section

I outlines ample leading indicators that confirm the magnitude of problems we face.

Governments have a chance to show true leadership and vision through creating national and regional skills strategies. An important contribution to redefining opportunities can flow out of our current dire state. The OECD framework on national skills strategy helps governments diagnose their current and future skills gaps. It estimates the social and economic impact of action and inaction[125]. For the government, the focus of action must remain on policy and strategy. Failure to anticipate future needs and to adapt the educational system to the new economy correctly is only one of the risks that could impact a nation's ability to overcome current challenges. The cost of failing to skill up the population is massive and is comprised of different elements (as discussed in Chapter #1: Realities of the Digital World). Yet the bottom line is straightforward. Educational institutions must begin to include updated content such as scientific, management and societal trends. They must follow new, participative pedagogies aimed at fostering critical thinking and innovative problem-solving through collaborative engagement with students.

A common diagnostic element is the problematic disconnection between the tertiary education system and the economy. Given the complexity of the current global economy, a set of high-level practical recommendations for universities will enable them to begin to adapt. Modifying degree curricula, business models and governance of universities to better fit our new world, are top priorities for governments that wish to maintain a sustainable tertiary education system. Yet the problem must be addressed at the primary and secondary school level as well. Some very interesting books published by specialists have decoded the weaknesses of the entire education system and made detailed recommendations to build a thriving 21st century education system.

Aligning the educational system to better upskill youth will not solve all the problems faced by society today. It is, however, an enormous piece of the puzzle when conceptualising solutions to reduce at-risk populations. Many of these low-skilled workers might have a degree or prefer to work in regions or sectors that are distressed. If nothing changes, their future is not bright. Degrees are no protection against unemployment. Today, unless a degree is in tech and includes international experience or is in a domain suffering from high job vacancies, it doesn't have the same market attractiveness as in the past. In addition, even if someone has an attractive degree, if they don't have the required behavioural skills, they will have difficulties finding a job. According to a variety of studies, CEOs are looking for behavioural skills which enable personal agility, strong communication, teamwork and a problem-solving mindset.

Companies have started to understand that an employee's capacity to learn and ability to acquire knowledge quickly, is now as important as their current knowledge or job-specific expertise. Learning on the job and being able to build out new features in one's role are winning characteristics in the work of the future. To some extent, through their learning capabilities and initiative, employees of the future will be expected to not only to define but evolve their job profile.

The education system, from primary school and beyond, must increase learning and teaching agility. Pedagogical effectiveness and efficiency will provide a better chance to have meaningful careers. Changing teaching methods and approaches will allow better development, and attractiveness, of STEM studies and careers, especially for at-risk populations (youths/women). Increased focus on the connection between educational content and marketplace needs will better orient students towards sustainable jobs.

Schools in Nature

Schools in Nature are just one excellent example of the evolution of teaching methods and focus. Eva Kätting, Director of Studies for the master's programme in Outdoor Environmental Education and Outdoor Life at Linköping University, in Sweden, wrote that teachers have a more complex role than just passing on information. *"They need to teach the students how to transform all this information into knowledge. In order to do that they [students] need practical experience."*

Schools in Nature use a specific pedagogy and trained teachers, supported by other organisations. In Sweden, the classrooms in nature approach is supported by the educational system[126]. More than 1,000 school teachers are trained every year. Interestingly, this method reinforces links with society and mobilises not-for-profit organisations that protect nature, to provide outdoor activities.

Parks and nature are exceptional locations to teach traditional academic subjects. In cities, schoolyards and parks are most accessible for outdoor teaching, so schoolyard design might require new conceptualisation. Experience in the outdoors has many benefits for young people's physical and mental abilities. It enhances their capacity to better understand scientific and technology issues[127]. Looking at the efficacy and variety of applications, this approach could make nature the main stage for STEM education. This would be a paradigm shift that could shake loose enormous potential.

Practical Recommendations for Universities

The 'how to learn' question must be fully revisited. Learning through nature, learning by doing, hybrid combinations of physical, social and digital processes are some of the most efficient ways to learn. We are entering an era in which innovation in pedagogy will increase educational effectiveness through multiple channels and also through increased personalisation of content and pro- grammes. New research, infrastructure and teachers' education are integral to success.

Generation Zs are already at university. What can be done in the short-term to increase employability and reduce the labour-market gap for them? This set of practical recommendations improves the link between universities and tomorrow's labour market. Over- all, the objective is to increase a university's agility, adapting the normal teaching timeframe to society's needs, and to move to a results-driven approach; creating university assets that are rele- vant and timely.

1. **Review governance: include private sector leaders on BoDs**

   Improved involvement between private sector leaders and the university's governance bodies allows strategy and underlying objectives to be more relevant to the labour market. University programmes can become more relevant to the market by:

   - adapting the curriculum

   - developing new partnerships with companies that provide a large portfolio of educational courses such as IBM or Cisco

   - undertaking joint applied research programmes

Universities might consider this to be undue external interference in their governance. Yet it is more of an assurance that these insti- tutions remain relevant to the market.

2. **Create a pedagogical innovation lab**

   The multitude of disciplines that can come together to form a high-value learning experience in technical, soft and digital domains is unlimited. Coupled with the students' profiles, access to online, on-the-job, and physical learning centres, can be powerful. This approach leverages emerging educational technology and sparks innovation. New research and experimentation regarding the skills acquisition process and relevant pedagogies can create more viable, productive and relevant university curricula.

The creation of innovation laboratories is a major strategic investment that allows the institution to keep up with change and improve their students' knowledge and skills acquisition process. The University of Luxembourg has just opened its learning centre; a technical innovation environment oriented towards digital learning and science. By offering wide access to many sources of high-quality knowledge via digital resources, the learning centre aims to better understand how to learn and teach.

3. **Introduce leadership, entrepreneurship and digital courses in all curricula**

   Although they are among the most in-demand skills, most syllabuses do not include entrepreneurship, leadership or digital courses. The need for their introduction is obvious, to allow students to better cope with market realities; increasing their long-term employability.

   The introduction of core and optional modules would accelerate students' introduction to the new economy or significantly complete their skills portfolio whatever their faculty or line of study. There is no need to recreate the wheel. Excellent content is available through many universities and organisations.

4. **Integrate practitioners to deliver in-demand topics**

   The most in-demand topics are evolving rapidly, and the corporate perspective is generally very different from the academic. For instance, many university digital and coding courses use programmes and standards which are obsolete.

In addition, there is a disconnect between what the market-place requires on a day-to-day basis and the theory that many universities provide.

When it comes to studying entrepreneurship, real entrepreneurs are the only credible role models and teachers. Some specialised degrees on entrepreneurship function without any true entrepreneurs as teachers. Including local entrepreneurs who can share their successes, failures and lessons learned, is a great way to increase the impact of the course. As entrepreneurship is so diverse, covering individuals, companies, government policy-makers, and social entrepreneurs, the university can rely on many truly experienced external people. Most students will only truly understand real leadership when the curriculum features experienced groups and company case studies lead by leaders from the field.

5. **Upskill teachers and professors**

Teachers, whether in primary schools or university, spend most of their working life in academia. Although many are recognised as experts in their field, few have acquired the facilitation knowledge or skill to involved and enthral their students in the learning experience. Upskilling teachers is important. It ensures that they are up-to-date on key relevant scientific, technological, business, and management domains and on the latest methods to engage students in their learning journey. The report, Energising and Employing America (2007), proposed that for a brighter future they needed to strengthen the skills of 250,000 teachers and professors[111]. This upskilling is required more than ever to improve the pedagogical effectiveness and the outcomes of teaching programmes, especially at the university level.

6. **Review the university business model**

Given the increasing competition between universities compelled to maintain investments in infrastructure, learning content, pedagogies and staff, a new model is needed to demonstrate their value and to share the risk. Most universities use tuition fee increases and/or extension of their programmes to increase their resources. They have clearly reached the limits of the model. Many students today have a problem with the length of a university programme. They know that it's possible to learn the same content in half the time, online or using some other form of condensed methodology.

The university success fee model is a very interesting trend. Initiated in 2014 on USA campuses, the success fee is based upon the student paying for quality. It aims to enhance the learning experience beyond the basic level of access secured by national and tuition funding. The fees are clearly linked to, and may only be increased, if the students are placed successful in well-paying jobs.

7. **Build a new generation vocational training unit**
   Universities are looking for new sources of revenues. The reform of vocational learning towards job-oriented training provides the opportunity to significantly increase activities that leverage all university assets.

   With a specific focus, adapted curricula and pedagogies, this new unit builds up partnerships with companies to license, deliver and distribute their own courses. Programmes are tailored to industries with investments in technology and machinery. Following the definition of requirements, the programme's condensed session are adapted to company and employee schedules. The university increases the value of their degrees and develops stronger relationships with the private sector. Companies and universities might also co-invest in technology to maximise usage. This closer collaboration on vocational training benefits programme quality, effectiveness, and therefore the students learning.

8. **Play a key role in the skills strategy**

   We have already recommended that government leaders launch a three- five- and ten-year skills strategy. The university can play a key role, in collaboration with business, in understanding the future needs of the territory and framing the results in new or revised curricula and vocational training. The territory's skills strategy is a great opportunity for university decision-makers to demonstrate their future value and to anticipate new needs. The university could develop a toolbox of future skills, open new education and research topics, and capture the related government and private budget.

Would universities become slaves to industry if they followed these recommendations? This might certainly be the first comment from university professors and deans, but we don't think this would happen. The university, rather isolated and insulated now, might better collaborate with the private sector and more easily meet the needs of students and society.

Main Messages

Education systems around the world are responsible for providing students with knowledge and skills that will equip them for a changing world. Although we can't completely forecast which jobs or capabilities the future will demand. We do know that in 2018, the top priority is tech and soft skills development. Few systems are actually equipping students for the workforce and society of the future.

The increased quality of e-learning is transforming talent development in the workplace; enabling a high number of employees to access any courses they wish. Radical updates to the educational system, from primary to tertiary-level schools, are the only way to support workers of the future and prepare them for a sustainable, meaningful and energizing future.

This is a paradigm shift for education policy-makers, who must create a dual track system that includes vocational training. We can no longer support low-impact training. It is a shift that must reach across to company subsidy policies. Organisations must shift thousands of euro being invested in tangible assets, to a more customised approach of intellectual capital asset investment, informed by the requirements or changes in fields impacting the workers' longevity. We have successful examples. The re-initiation of apprenticeship programmes coupled with a new business col-laboration model, is taking place in Germany now. We must learn from these successes to create a platform of life-long learning and upskilling excellence.

Chapter 12: Conclusion

This book provides innovative, ambitious and practical solutions to rapidly and significantly increase the skills portfolio of the untapped talent pool that exists in virtually every company, sector or country. It provides a path for upskilling workforces that will create a vibrant and exciting future and feed sustainable growth, employability and social inclusion.

The acceleration of the digital economy is challenging companies in North America and Europe. Hundreds of millions overqualified, under-skilled unemployed workers no longer have what is needed in the marketplace today. Talent pools are becoming more homogenous and smaller. Indeed, women, as only one example, lag in major, higher-paid and -skilled categories; STEM, the boardroom, management, technology. Companies must shift their thinking about resources and be ready to optimise value from diverse staff working side by side.

These lost workforces are causing an incredible loss of growth. It is time for communities of practice to coalesce around the diversity and equality imperatives. We no longer have the latitude to waste valuable resource pools.

Businesses are hampered by their inability to find the right resources. Corporations are desperately looking for adequate profiles to fill the growing number of job vacancies. Many sectors are faltering as they endeavour to transition their business model, and workforce, to the future. Corporations must be willing and able to compete in the evolving digital landscape.

Some have clearly understood this and are making changes. Yet few corporations are proactively dealing with this challenge.

The market understands, and this, in part, is driving the booming HR Tech eco-system, which is one of the hottest growth areas in business. Venture Capitalists demonstrate a clear appetite for this sector as they invest in thousands of HR start-ups and solutions. The volume of investment shows that there is no foreseeable slow-down for this market in the near- or medium-term.

As the technology eco-system steps up to provide innovative HR solutions, the whole cycle of personnel acquisition and management can now be supported and energised. Yet without being alarmist, we must flag that the lack of competent resources is becoming more important each day. In the very near future, it is sure to bring HR even farther into the spotlight. Some of HR's greatest challenges today include fostering the evolution of competencies that will allow workers to remain employable and efficient. This requires more targeted training investments.

For most corporations, filling the competency gap is an ongoing activity. The previous approach to training was to provide inadequate amounts of untargeted training to, in many cases, the wrong population. Corporations must take a focused and intense approach to upskilling. They must apply training budgets to those categories of workers who are most at-risk. By aligning training and upskilling plans with technology installations or upgrades, organisations can maximise programme effectiveness and efficiency.

What few organisations are discussing is the imperative to upskill HR teams; to ensure they understand the technologies that will impact their employee population… and how technology will change the way they do their job. We are in the Industry 4.0 revolution, but we need HR 5.0 to guide policy and processes, and to set standards that will ensure viable and sustainable jobs for the future.

CEOs and the executive team must realise their responsibility.

This book clearly demonstrates the financial merit and efficacy of upskilling; to do any less is to be delinquent in their duties. Lacking the foresight to create an upskilling environment, means that the C-Suite has failed to fulfil its strategic value.

The war for talent is stronger than ever. The social, economic and financial magnitude of preparing the workforce for future jobs … globally, is daunting. Countries without the appropriate digital infra-structures and well-prepared workforce may become 'no-go' zones for the international community as their growth stalls or slows, and their businesses downsize. Countries with visionary leaders are designing ecosystems that enable the marketplace to adapt to the digital economy and help put the unemployed to work. They will thrive; producing more entrepreneurs and attracting investment, which will generate more endogenous growth.

We already see business, the government and society encour-aging the design of new innovative solutions for implementing upskilling, updating their educational and vocational training sys-tems, and leveraging local potential.

We are in this together. Be part of the revolution. Read this book and then share these concepts with two people and another two people. Gather insight and momentum. Take action with your peers, colleagues and community. By exchanging views and in-formation on this topic, you will attract people and opinions. Don't be afraid to further develop your own perspective on the positive opportunities and options for solving this approaching global crisis in your own community.

Appendix

References

This section contains reference to studies, reports, white papers and websites that we used during our research. To stay up to date with our latest writing or to connect with us regarding your project or initiative, please check out our webpage: www.pwc.lu/en/upskilling-for-competitiveness-and-employability.html

1. Philips, M., It's not a Skills Gap: U.S. Workers are overqualified and Undertrained', Bloomberg, August 19, 2014

2. 'Putting faces to the jobs at risk of automation, Policy Brief on the Future of Work', *OECD*, March 2018

3. 'The Anxious Optimist in the Corner Office', PwC, 2018

4. Arntz, M., Gregory, T., & Zierahn, U., 'The Risk of Automation for Jobs in OECD Countries: A Comparative Analysis', *OECD Social, Employment and Migration Working Papers, No. 189*, OECD Publishing, Paris

5. 'Quarterly National Accounts: Quarterly Growth Rates of real GDP, change over previous quarter', OECD. Stat, accessed August 2018

6. 'The Growth of Europe', European Commission, Brussels, 2017

7. 'Transformative Technologies and Jobs of the Future', OECD Secretary General, March 27, 2018

8. Frey, C. B., Osborne, M. A., 'The Future Of Employment: How Susceptible Are Jobs To Computerisation?', Oxford, September 17, 2013

9. Survey of Adult Skills (PIAAC), OECD Publishing, Paris., March 2018, p. 131

10. ;World Population Ageing 2017 – Highlights', United Nations, Department of Economic and Social Affairs, Population Division (ST/ESA/SER.A/397), 2017

11. 'Pensions at a Glance 2017', OECD.Stat, November 14, 2018

12. Jaruzelski, B., Staack, V., & Chwalik, R ., 'Will Stronger Borders Weaken Innovation', Strategy +Business, October 24, 2017

13. Mclvor, J., Free tuition for EU students in Scotland extended to 2019-2020, BBC News 1 Feb, 2018

14. 'Japan Unemployment Rate', Statistics Japan, Trading Economies, October 30, 2018

15. 'Towards a Reskilling Revolution', World Economic Forum in collaboration with The Boston Consulting Group, Switzerland, 2018

16. 'Eight Futures of Work', World Economic Forum in collaboration with The Boston Consulting Group, Switzerland, 2018

17. 'Future of work, A journey to 2022', PwC, Human Capital, 2014

18. 'The new CFO Mandate: Prioritize, transform, repeat' McKinsey, Future of Work, December 2018

19. Garton, E., 'Firm of the Future: Workforce of the Future', Bain & Company, July 13, 2017

20. 'Norwegian Strategy for Skills Policy 2017-2021', Norwegian Government, 2017, p. 12

21. Beltempo, C., 'Canada launches new Global Skills Strategy', Norton, Rose, Fulbright, June 2017

22. 'Proposal for a Council Recommendation on Key Competencies for Life Long Learning', EU Commission, January 1, 2018

23. Fain, P., 'White House Council on Reskilling Challenge', Inside Higher ED, July 19, 2018, p. 17

24. 'CEA Report: Addressing America's Reskilling Challenge', Council of Economic Advisors, July 17, 2018

25. 'What is SkillsFuture?' Government of Singapore, 2017

26. 'German vocational training and education cooperation', Kultusminister Konferenz; 2017 p. 6

27. The talent challenge: rebalancing skills for the digital age, PwC, 21st CEO Survey, talent, 2018

28. 'Unemployment rates EU-28 EA-19 US and Japan season-ally adjusted January 2000 July 2018.png', Eurostat, July 2018

29. 'Unemployment Rates, Seasonally Adjusted', Eurostat, Statistics Explained, July 2018

30. Diosadado, B., 'The Price Of Vacancy: The Cost Of Unfilled Technology Jobs', Forbes, June 22, 2017

31. 'Job vacancy statistics', Eurostat, Statistics Explained, September 2018

32. Employment rate by educational attainment, Eurostat, October 24, 2018

33. Employment rate by level of education, age group 25-64, 1993-2016 (%).png, Eurostat, Statistics Explained, July 2017

34. 'How many young are not in employment, education or training?', CEDEFOP, February 01, 2018

35. 'The Future of Jobs Report 2018', World Economic Forum, Centre for the New Economy and Society, 2018

36. 'Luxembourg: Skills forecasts up to 2025', CEDEOP, 2015

37. Laouchez, J-M., et al., '2030: The 8.5 Trillion Talent Short-age, Korn Ferry Institute, May 9, 2017

38. Morath, E., 'Workers' Pay Rises at Fastest Rate in a De-cade', The Wall Street Journal, October 31, 2018

39. 'Rapport D'Activite 2017', Government of Luxembourg, Ministere du Travail, de l'Emploie et de l'Economie sociale et solidaire, 2017

40. Geissbauer, R., et al, 'Global Digital Operations Study, PwC, 2018', PwC, Digital Champions, 2018

41. 'Skills Outlook 2017: Skills and Global Value Chains', OECD Education, May 4, 2017

42. Chor, D., 'Unpacking Sources of Comparative Advantage: A Quantitative Approach', Singapore Management Univer-sity, Research Collection School of Economics, October, 2008

43. Morrison, A., Pietrobelli, C., & Rabellotti, R., 'Global value chains and technological capabilities', Oxford Development Studies. (2008). pp. 36. 39-58

44. 'EU : Adult participation in life-long learning is stagnant', European Commission, EPALE, Newsroom, November 16, 2016

45. 'Hours of training per employee in the training industry in the United states from 2016 to 2018, by company size', Statista, 2018

46. 'Exploitation des declarations fiscales 24-83' Cereq, 2009

47. Beraud, D., 'L'évaluation des formations par les entreprises et les salariés, Net.doc .137', Cereq, May 2015

48. 'L'accès à la formation des salariés du secteur privé en 2016', INFPC, Observatoire de la formation, November 2017

49. Kurzweil, K., 'The Singularity is Near', Viking, NY, p. 47

50. 'Hiring Could be Even More Difficult in 2018 as Employers Compete for a Shrinking Talent Pool, Compensation, Hiring & Recruiting', HR Daily Advisor, Feb 28, 2018

51. 'Solving the Talent Shortage', Manpower Group May, 2018, p. 5

52. Macfarlane, A., 'Japan Needs more workers and it can't find them', CNN Business, May 30, 2017

53. Cambecedes, F., 'Les 600 startups de la Galaxie ~HRTech!', #rmsnews, June 2017

54. Qiu, J., 'HR tech is evolving quickly – more acquisitions are on the way', VenturBeat, July 14, 2018

55. Polack, E., 'New Cigna Study Reveals Loneliness At Epidemic Levels In America', Cigna, May 01, 2018

56. The Power of Parity, McKinsey & Company, September 2015

57. 'End Poverty, Annual Report 2017', World Bank Group, 2017

58. 'PwC Spotlight on: Gender Diversity', PwC Global, 2017

59. 'PwC's making diversity a reality', The Gender Agenda, PwC Blog, July 30, 2018

60. 'Nudging Women into Tech' PwC Global, July 30, 2018

61. 'Women In Science, Technology, Engineering, And Mathematics (STEM)', Catalyst, Knowledge Center, Jan 3, 2018

62. 'Future Works Skills 2020', University of Phoenix, Institute for the Future, 2011

63. Austin, R., & Pisano, G., 'Neurodiversity as a competitive advantage', May-June 2017

64. Profeldt, E., 'Are We Ready for a Workforce that is 50% Freelance?', Forbes, October 17, 2017

65. 'Freelancing in America: 2017', Edelman Intelligence, Upskill & Freelncer's Union, September 2017

66. 'Future of Work', European Commission, European Political Strategy Centre, June 10, 2016

67. Williams, M., et al, 'The True Diversity of Self-Employment', CSRE, 2017, p. 14

68. 'Employment Statistics', European Commission, Eurostat, Statistics Explained, 2018

69. 'Workforce of the Future – the competing forces shaping 2030', PwC Global, 2017

70. 'Nordea to cut at least 6,000 jobs in fight to stay competitive', Bloomberg, October 26, 2017

71. 'Nordea to axe 6,000 jobs in drive to digital future', Financial Times (FT), October 26, 2017

72. 'Nordea is axing a fifth of its work force', Business Insider Nordic, October, 27, 2017

73. 'ING plans to cut 7,000 job, spend on digital draws union ire', Reuters, 3 October 2016

74. 'Japan's banks plan 33,000 job cuts in digital downsizing', Finextra Research, 31 October 2017

75. Sainato, M., 'They're liquidating us': AT&T continues layoffs and outsourcing despite profits', August 28, 2018

76. Campbell, A., O'Connor, L., New York Daily News Layoffs Ax Half The Newsroom Staff, July 23, 2018

77. Concha, J., 'New York Daily News cuts half its editorial staff in latest downsizing', The Hill, July 23, 2018

78. 'The Bottom line - necessity of training your managers', HRProfessional Magazine,

79. '2017 Training Industry Report', Training Magazine, 2017

80. 'Building the workforce of tomorrow, today', McKinsey, November 2018, [online] accessed November 2018

81. Gumbel, P., & Reich, A., 'Building the workforce of tomorrow, today', McKinsey Quarterly, November 2018

82. 'Global Women's Leader' Task Force Creating the Climate to Win', IBM Corporation, Catalyst Knowledge Center, Jan 6, 2000

83. 'New supportive service launched for businesses across the Sheffield City Region', Sheffield City Region, Media Releases, April 27, 2016

84. Norriss, P., 'SPONSORED: £17m funding for Skills Bank to boost fortunes of local firms', The Star, March 31, 2017

85. 'SCR Businesses rush to Growth Hub's free Masterclasses before it's too late', Sheffield City Region, News, October 24, 2018

86. '2018 Best Coding Bootcamps', Switchup, November 2018

87. Heidsieck, L., 'Le boom des écoles du web pour apprendre le code informatique', Le Figaro, June 05, 2017

88. ;Japan's Online Start-up School', The Bridge, 24 October, 2017

89. '2018 How much do enterprises invest in continuing vocational training – in purchasing power parities', CEDEFOP, February 1, 2018

90. 'Why invest in employment', European Federation for Services to Individuals, December 2012

91. 'Jobs in Photonics', Epic-association, October 2018

92. 'La formation des demandeurs d'emploi', Cour des Comptes, France, May 2018

93. 'Getting Skills Right', OECDiLibrary, December 6, 2017

94. 'Canada Jobs Grant - Training Grants for Human Resources Development', MentorWorks, 2018

95. 'CRÉDIT-ADAPTATION', Le Forem, 2018

96. 'About Skills Future', Skills Future, 2017

97. 'Programmes for You', SkillsFuture, 2017

98. 'Course Fee and Absentee Payroll Funding for Employers', Singapore Government, 2018

99. 'What we Do' National Skills Development, 2018

100. 'ABOUT UPSKILL CAPITAL', Upskilling Capital, 2018

101. 'Which Member States have the largest share of EU's GDP?', European Commission, Eurostat August 2018

102. 'Koto-SIB', Epiquis, 2018

103. 'Investment Plan for Europe: First social impact bond scheme in Europe supports integration in Finland', European Investment Fund, June 2, 2017,

104. '125,000 Disney Employees to Receive $1,000 Cash Bonus and Company Launches New $50 Million Higher Education Program', Walt Disney Company, January 23, 2018

105. 'Annual Impact Investor Survey', GINN, 2018, p. 13

106. Mon Compte Activite, Un Seul Site, Government of France, Public Service

107. 'Annual Impact Survey', GINN, 2018

108. D. Kelley, S. Singer, & M. Herrington, '2011 Global Report', Global Entrepreneur Monitor, 2011, p. 10

109. 'Global Report', GEM, GERA, 2018

110. 'Software Impact Report', BSA foundation, September 2017

111. 'Rising Above the Gathering Storm: Energizing and Employing America for a Brighter Economic Future', NAP, Washington, DC, 2007

112. 'Europe needs more leaders with strong technical skills', European Commission, Internal Market, Industry, Entrepre-

neurship and SMEs, February 02, 2017

113. 'The high-tech skills gap in Europe will reach 500,000 in 2025 with a strong polarisation of skills needed', e-Leadership, 2015

114. 'What is the 'T'?', T-Summit, T-Academy, 2018

115. McNaboe, J., et al., 'National Skills Bulletin', National Skills Council, December 2017

116. 'Ireland's National Skills Strategy 2025', Department of Education and Skills, p.114

117. 'Fast-track – a quicker introduction of newly arrived immigrants', Government Offices of Sweden, Ministry of Employment, October 2016

118. Svensson, B., 'Drygt 4 miljoner kronor till den trärelaterade industrin i Småland, Tracemtrum', Tracentrum

119. 'Kompetenz-und Qualifierungsbedarfe bis 2030, Bundesministerium für Arbeit and Soziales', Federal Ministry of Labor and Social Affairs, September 2017

120. 'Department for International Trade, 'Trade White Paper: Preparing for our future UK trade policy, Government Response', January 2018, p. 13

121. McGuinness, D., 'How a cyberattack transformed Estonia', BBC, April 27, 2017

122. 'Competitive Council Configuration', European Council, Consilium, June 26, 2018

123. J. Lessor, R. Phillips & N. Cassidy, 'Reimagining the Police Workforce', Accenture, 2018

124. Nedelkoska, L. and G. Quintini (2018), 'Automation, skills use and training', OECD Social, Employment and Migration Working Papers, No. 202, OECD Publishing, Paris,

125. 'National Skills Strategy', OECD, 2018

126. McGurk, L., In Sweden, Teaching Outside Is In, Children & Nature Network, October 23, 2015

127. Morris, N., 'What does the research say about Outdoor Learning? ', OPENspace Research Centre, English Outdoor Council, 2003

Acroynyms

AGV	Automatic Guided Vehicles
AI	Artificial Intelligence
AR	Augmented Reality
BAC	Baccalaureate
CDO	Chief Digital Officer
CEDEFOP	Centre for the Development of Vocational Training
CEO	Chief Executive Officer
CJG	Canada Job Grant
CO2	Carbon Dioxide
CRM	Customer Relationship Management
CSR	Customer Service Relationship
CVT	Continuing Vocational Training
CVTS	Continuing Vocational Training Survey
DM	Developed Markets
ECB	European Central Bank
EIB	European Investment Bank
EM	Emerging Markets
EPIC	European Photonics Industry Consortium
EPSCO	Employment, Social Policy, Health and Consumer Affairs Council
ERP	Enterprise Resources Planning
EU	European Union
EU28	European Union 28 countries
FTE	Full-time Employee
GDP	Gross Domestic Product
GDPR	General Data Protection Regulations
GEM	Global Entrepreneurship Monitor
Gen X	Generation X (1965 - 1979)
Gen Y	Generation Y or Millennials (born between 1980 and 1994)
Gen Z	Generation Z (1995 and 2010)
GIIN	Global Impact Investing Network
GVC	Global Value Chain

HK	Hong Kong
HQ	Head Quarters
HR	Human Resources
HRD	Human Resources Director Magazine
ICT	Internet, Communication, Technology
IoT	Internet of Things
IT	Internet Technology
LGBT	Lesbian, Gay, Bi- and Transgender
M&A	Mergers and Acquisitions
Millennial	Or Generation Y born between 1980-1994
MOOCs	Massive Open Online Learning
MSDE	Ministry of Skill Development & Entrepreneurship
MVP	Minimum Viable Product
NEET	Not in Employment, Education or Training
NSDC	National Skill Development Corporation
NYSE	New York Stock Exchange
OECD	Organisation for Economic Co-operation and Development
PISA	Programme for International Student Assessment
ROI	Return on Investment
RPA	Robotic Process Automation
SIMO	Skills India Mission Operation
SMEs	Small and Medium-sized Enterprises
STEM	Science, Technology, Engineering, Medicine
TMT	Technology, media, and telecoms
UAE	Unite Arab Emirates
UIB	Upskilling Impact Bond
UK	United Kingdom
UNFPA	The United Nations Population Fund
US / USA	United States of America
VC	Venture Capitalists
WF	Workforce
WFP	Work Force Planning
WFSP	Workforce Skills Planning

Notes

Notes

Notes

Notes

Notes

Notes

9 781912 850662